SENIOR C.
APPOINTMENTS

A Review of the Methods of Appointment of
Area and Suffragan Bishops, Deans, Provosts,
Archdeacons and Residentiary Canons

The Report of the Working Party established by the Standing
Committee of the General Synod of the Church of England

*This Report has only the authority of the Working Party which
prepared it.*

CHURCH HOUSE PUBLISHING
Church House, Great Smith Street, London SW1P 3NZ

ISBN 07151 3746 8

GS 1019
Published 1992 for the General Synod of the Church of England
by Church House Publishing

© *The Central Board of Finance of the Church of England 1992*

Printed in England by Tasprint

CONTENTS

		Page
Chairman's Preface		v
1	Introduction	1
2	Some Ecclesiological Principles	6
3	Comments and Suggestions Received	9
4	The Case for Change	12
5	Advice to the Sovereign	20
6	Proposals for Change	
	Suffragan Bishops	35
	Deans and Provosts	38
	The Process and the Role of the Appointing Groups	42
	Archdeacons	46
	Residentiary Canons	49
7	Implementation and Cost Implications	52

Appendices

| I | Origins, Terms of Reference, Membership, Comments, Meetings, and Suggestions Invited | 55 |
| II | Current Processes for making Appointments to Posts within the Working Party's Remit | 61 |

III Two Papers by Professor Henry Chadwick:
    i.   Church Leadership in History and Theology   75
    ii. Some Theological and Historical
        Considerations   89

IV A Paper by the Provost of Sheffield:
    Making Appointments in the Church   99

V The Motion carried by the General Synod in July
   1974, and the Prime Minister's Statement to the
   House of Commons on 8 June 1976 concerning the
   Appointment of Diocesan Bishops   107

VI Guidelines for Appointing Groups   111

VII Memorandum of Dissent   115
    by Mr Frank Field, MP

CHAIRMAN'S PREFACE

The Report here presented is unanimous, save for Mr Frank Field, MP. Any reservation by any member of the Working Party is important. But let no one underestimate the significance of a report otherwise agreed by such a wide range of churchmanship, background and approach.

The Report in 1970 of our predecessors, the Church and State Commission, was qualified by no less than four of its members by way of a memorandum of dissent, additional notes thereto, and a separate note of dissent. However, happily, the members of the Commission saw virtually all their proposals implemented, and it would therefore not be too optimistic to hope that ours would be also.

Our proposals are essentially not revolutionary but evolutionary. They build on the experience of the fairly recent past, but of necessity they break entirely new ground. They deal with matters of considerable delicacy. They make proposals for changes in fields which have so far been left untouched. They unashamedly depend upon balance. Balance, that is, between the strengths of the existing methods of appointment on the one hand and the benefits of greater openness on the other.

But above all they are designed for a Church which retains a national role and which is not just a sect. In such a Church there must be room for the public interest to be expressed. Nothing in these proposals diminishes the national position of the Church and it is in that spirit that they are brought forward.

The Report has taken time to produce. It was in the autumn of 1987 that the Standing Committee extended invitations to my colleagues and myself to undertake this work. Almost immediately, I was responsible for delay by the need for unexpected surgery, the cause of which thankfully turned out to be benign. Consequently the Working Party only held its first meeting on 17 June 1988. For this particular delay only I am responsible, however inadvertently.

Our work was greatly assisted by two parliamentarians, Mr Ian Gow, MP, and Charles, Lord Williams of Elvel. To the horror of the whole nation Mr Ian Gow was assassinated on 30 July 1990, two years into our work. It is impossible to describe the sense of loss which my colleagues and I felt, and continue to feel. All of us will long remember the morning upon which we corporately remembered him in the Rutland Chapel of St George's Chapel, Windsor. In the autumn of that year, though happily for a very pleasant reason, we lost Charles, Lord Williams of Elvel who was elected as Deputy Leader of the Labour Party in the House of Lords. Both had contributed greatly to our proceedings, both had read themselves deeply into the subject.

Given the nature of our enquiry, it was absolutely essential that they be replaced. However the necessary consultations took time, and it was only at our meeting on 20 March 1991, that is to say little over a year ago, that we could be joined by Mr Roger Sims, MP, and Mr Frank Field, MP. Both have been absolutely invaluable, and we particularly recognise the burden we placed upon them by asking them to read themselves into the subject when we were already a long way into our draft report. It is no possible criticism of them to say that we necessarily had to 'tread water' a little to allow them to catch up, and frankly to do anything less would have been both discourteous and wasteful of their expertise. We are deeply grateful to them for undertaking the task, but there is no denying that these events slowed us up. We had already added to our burden of work by ourselves suggesting at our first meeting that our terms of reference should be widened to include the method of appointment of Archdeacons. This was subsequently agreed by the Standing Committee and we were greatly strengthened by the appointment from December 1988 of the Archdeacon of Exeter.

Finally, we were extremely conscious in our early days of the work of the Archbishops' Group on the Episcopate 1990. This was after all a Commission working in our field and it seemed foolish for us to get too far into our work without knowing how it would report. But this Commission also took longer to report than was expected. It is no discourtesy to that Commission to say that, when it reported, it really affected our particular work very little.

No words can express the appreciation we feel for the expertise which has been available to us, and upon which we have freely drawn, of our distinguished Assessors. Above all, we are indebted to Mr N. D. Barnett of the General Synod Office, assisted from

September 1990 by Mr P. A. W. Hopkins. At times their tasks have seemed overwhelming and we are acutely aware of the pressures which we have placed upon them.

This leads me respectfully to suggest that the General Synod, before setting up enquiries like ours, needs to have greater regard to the pressures to which this subjects their staff. The permanent staff is very small by any measure. An additional responsibility like this one is proportionately the greater. Whenever a particular problem arises, the temptation is always to appoint a committee to look into it; but the burden of proof in such a case is surely on those who require it. One of their main considerations ought to be the demands which such an enquiry makes upon the permanent staff.

For myself I look back on the past years of intense work and thought with genuine pleasure. I rejoice in friendships made and retained. I have been enriched by the experiences and thoughts of all my colleagues, to whom I express my grateful thanks.

July 1992   William van Straubenzee
                                                                Chairman

1

INTRODUCTION

1.1 The background leading up to our appointment as a Working Party, our detailed terms of reference and membership, together with those individuals and groups from whom we invited comments and suggestions are set out in Appendix I to this Report.

1.2 We were asked to review the method of appointment of area and suffragan bishops, deans, provosts and residentiary canons of cathedrals and (subsequently) of archdeacons. We were not therefore concerned with the arrangements for the appointment of diocesan bishops, stipendiary or honorary assistant bishops, deans and canons of Royal Peculiars (which are extraprovincial as well as extradiocesan), or of minor or honorary canons of cathedrals.

1.3 In the course of our discussions two issues about 'conditions of service' were raised. The first was whether the offices with which we were to be concerned should continue to be freehold offices. The second was whether it was appropriate that there should continue to be stipend differentials. We have not sought ourselves to examine these questions in any detail. To do so would have taken us beyond our terms of reference. We welcome however the fact that in January 1991 the General Synod carried a motion in the following terms:

> That this Synod consider that the freehold tenure of all ecclesiastical offices should be reviewed, with consideration being given to its replacement by a renewable term of years, and accordingly request the Standing Committee to provide for such a review and to report to the General Synod.

In the light of that motion, and of the debate on conditions of service in the Joint Meeting of the Convocations in February 1990, the Standing Committee of the General Synod appointed a Group 'to co-ordinate the consideration of issues relating to clergy conditions of service, including a review of the ecclesiastical freehold . . .' The issues to be considered will, we understand, include also the question of stipend differentials.

1.4   Before formulating and agreeing the recommendations we now make we were concerned to be informed fully about the present legal provisions governing the methods of appointment which we were asked to review and about the present processes under which those legal requirements are met. It was one of the underlying themes reflected, both explicitly and implicitly, in the letters we received that the present processes, if not also the present formal legal provisions, were not widely known or understood. Indeed we found that we ourselves had much to learn about how these appointments are made.

1.5   We set out in some detail in Appendix II the present legal provisions for appointments to those offices with which we are concerned together with a description of the processes leading up to the final appointment in each case.

1.6   The essence of the present arrangements is the freedom of the diocesan bishop and the Crown respectively in deciding how to fill a vacant post. Thus, for example, a diocesan bishop is not required to go through any specific procedures in the choosing of a suffragan apart from the submission of a petition to the Sovereign. We understand that it is nowadays normal practice that he will consult his provincial Archbishop, not least because the latter may have to consecrate the prospective bishop, but the sole specific requirement is the petition to the Sovereign proposing two possible names for the appointment. The petition is submitted through the Prime Minister who by long-standing custom and practice always recommends the first name. When he comes to choose an archdeacon or appoint to a residentiary canonry in his gift, the diocesan bishop's power of appointment is total.

1.7   The Crown has similar freedom in appointing to deaneries, to those canonries which are in its gift, and to those provostships, archdeaconries and canonries which revert to it when the priest in question becomes a diocesan bishop. It acts in like manner when the diocesan see is vacant since a bishop's patronage lapses to the Crown in those circumstances. Any change in this arrangement would require an amendment of the law.

1.8 In practice, although the steps taken vary from diocese to diocese and from appointment to appointment, bishops are consulting increasingly widely about the requirements of the post to be filled, and the kind of person who would be suitable. Many consult their bishop's council when a suffragan see is vacant and/or the relevant rural or area deaneries when an archdeacon is needed, as well as individuals such as the chairmen of the houses of clergy and laity. Others seek views from a range of other people informally. Among the many factors they take into account are the need for a balance of views, of experience and of churchmanship tradition among the senior staff of the diocese. Enquiries about specific names are rather more circumspect and many bishops, anxious about the damage that can be caused by rumours and leaks (not least to those named and their families), confine their investigations to a small number of close and trusted colleagues or officials, and other bishops.

1.9 Similarly, the Crown consults extensively. In appointing a new dean, for example, it aims to balance and if possible satisfy the respective needs of the cathedral, the diocese and the local community and, where relevant, the national needs. The consultation is carried out by the Prime Minister's Secretary for Appointments and his practice is to seek the views of the diocesan bishop, the residentiary canons, the greater chapter, lay officials and members of the congregation, as well as people in leadership roles in the local community. He will discuss the names of candidates with the diocesan bishop and give particular weight to the bishop's suggestions, while reserving the rights of the Crown in the making of the ultimate decision. The Church is appreciative of the services of successive holders of that office over many years.

1.10 The services of the Archbishops' Appointments Secretary and his office are available when any of these posts is to be filled. He plays a limited part in the filling of Crown posts, although he will often assist a bishop with his preliminary thinking. He is on occasion consulted by the Crown. He invariably assists in all other instances: on the rare occasion that he is not consulted by a bishop who has a vacancy, he will take the initiative. He does so because an important part of his role is to draw to the attention of bishops making appointments possible candidates in other dioceses, with the aim of building up the strength of the leadership of the Church as a whole as well as of the particular diocese.

1.11 To be able to do this he must gather information continuously – in both formal and informal ways – about clergy of appropriate gifts, those who others think have it in them to fill with distinction, either now or in the future, posts which are the subject of this Working Party's concern (see also paras. 51-57 of Appendix II).

1.12 In the letters we received, two of the underlying general concerns expressed were, first that the process leading up to an appointment should be an open one (in the sense that the process itself should be in the public realm) and second that such open processes should ensure that wide consultations took place in a regular and structured way.

1.13 A number of helpful suggestions were made to us about how these general concerns might best be expressed in practice. In considering these suggestions, and in formulating the recommendations we now make, we have had in mind a number of considerations.

1.14 The Church of England is by law established. It is a Church which has a presence in all parts of the country and has the privilege and opportunity to offer a ministry to all. In its particular form of establishment it is a Church which, under the Crown and Parliament, is both episcopal and synodical.

1.15 The balance to be struck between these factors in the matter of the method of appointment to those offices with which we are concerned is, we believe, best expressed by leaving the decisive voice with the diocesan bishop but ensuring that the diocesan bishop exercises his voice in the light of an established and recognised procedure and following wide prior consultations.

In the proposals we make in Chapter 6 we have sought appropriately to reflect that view.

1.16   In our recommendations we set out the kind of consultations which we believe should take place. In doing so we reflect

i.   the balance we believe to be appropriate in each case between the Church's local and national interest,

ii.   the interest of those outside as well as within the formal synodical structures, and

iii.   the importance of drawing into the process contributions from the wider community.

1.17   A number of the appointments with which we have been concerned are ones which are ultimately made by the Sovereign on the advice of the Prime Minister. In Chapter 5 we discuss some questions about the route by which the Sovereign receives advice on these appointments.

2

SOME ECCLESIOLOGICAL PRINCIPLES

2.1 In conducting our review we have had in mind some general theological considerations and reflections about the nature of office in the Church. Our reflections have been much aided by papers prepared for us by the Revd Professor Henry Chadwick and by the Provost of Sheffield. We reproduce their papers to us as Appendix III and Appendix IV to our Report respectively.

2.2 It is possible to discern some strands of ecclesiological principle emerging from the Church's tradition, although we can obtain no clear guidance from biblical sources as to methods of appointment, and these have in practice varied considerably during the history of the Church:

i. the primary pattern of ministry is given by Our Lord himself, who came not to be ministered to but to minister and give his life as a ransom for many;

ii. appointment to office in the Church is not just about investing someone with symbols of authority. It is a calling by God through his Church, the body of Christ. Moreover the authority imparted embodies the Gospel principle of service;

iii. the pastoral care of the flock, the proclamation of the Gospel, the safeguarding of authentic teaching and ethical discipline are inherent in the apostolic commission;

iv. reviewing the development of the early Church, the permanence of certain functions within the life of the Church passed into the nature of an order within the structure of the Church. However, although replicated in the wider Church, none of these orders of ministry had an existence apart from the community which it was called to serve. So the ecumenical council of Chalcedon laid down that a clergyman should be ordained for a specific pastoral task in a named place rather than in vacuo;

v. the early Church laid emphasis on the role of local clergy and laity in choosing their bishop, their choice being validated by the involvement of other bishops in the consecration representing the interest of the wider Church. That involvement of clergy and laity reflects the ecclesiological principle that bishops, clergy and laity together make up the Church, as well as making practical sense in terms of helping to secure support for leadership;

vi. the functions of the church leader have always included representing the community he serves in the widest sense as well as ministering to it;

vii. the Holy Spirit bestows on the community diverse and complementary gifts. All members are called to discover with the help of the community the gifts they have received and to use them for the building up of the Church and for the service of the world to which the Church is sent.

Implications

2.3 These principles seem to have implications for methods of appointment in the Church e.g:

the implication that the methods of appointment should be sensitive to local concerns and the needs of the community served by the post in question;

the suggestion that the interests of the local community outside the Church as well as those of the local Church should be taken into account in the process of appointment;

the suggestion that the interests of the whole Church must be taken into account in the procedure for his appointment. A church leader is not simply a figure in the local community but a representative of that community to the wider world, including the wider Church. A bishop, for instance, holds an order of ministry in and for the whole Church.

2.4 The combination of a number of interests in such

appointments argues that the process through which they are made will only be effective if it permits wide access and open discussion. The procedures should encourage the discovery and harnessing of the different gifts available within and to the Church. Moreover those making decisions about appointments must be known. Procedures must embody Christian values. They should be fair and just, for example, and not permit preferential treatment, prejudice or discrimination.

2.5   Methods of appointment should be consistent with the tradition of the Church but not hide-bound by it. Above all, they should be open to the activity of the Holy Spirit. God's choice may often prove unexpected but the processes by which his choice appears should be of the very best – nothing else is worthy either of him or of those involved in the process. So the insights to be gained from secular appointments practice – the use of job descriptions, systems of appraisal, advertising, carefully moni-tored short-listing, and rigorous interviewing checked against references, for example – are not irrelevant secular fashions but potentially useful tools to be gathered and utilised to assist in the achievement of God's purpose. Appointment procedures are not simply matters of bureaucratic management and administration, but an integral and essential part of realising the Church's whole mission and ministry.

3

COMMENTS AND SUGGESTIONS RECEIVED

3.1 From the outset the Working Party felt it important that its own deliberations should be informed by contributions from others. While we did not commission a formal survey of opinion, a wide range of people was invited to contribute, and a general invitation was issued through national and provincial newspapers. Further details of the people from whom contributions were invited are given in Appendix I.

3.2 The nature of the submissions received (283 of which were letters) was varied, ranging from very brief personal comment to lengthy and detailed proposals. Many of the submissions reflected personal experiences. Those which made proposals for reforming the present system mostly confined comment to one specific group of senior church appointments. Relatively few contributors attempted to identify a set of principles that should govern the system of appointments generally, though the same specific suggestions were often made by more than one writer.

3.3 There was therefore limited scope for identifying common strands with any degree of confidence. Not all comments and suggestions made were calls for change; a number argued for the status quo. However the *general points* that were raised, and which were within our terms of reference, included:

a plea for less secrecy concerning the methods of appointment, and for wider consultation in making the appointments;

a concern that the diocesan bishop should retain the decisive say in his senior appointments;

a concern that the field of potential candidates for appointment should be drawn more widely;

a need for better 'career planning' or 'ministry development' in the Church, including for instance 'sideways moves' for suffragan bishops;

a concern for more attention to be paid to the compilation of job descriptions;

an encouragement for improved methods of appraisal of an individual's ministry;

a call for advertising to be permitted in some senior appointments;

a concern that, before an appointment was made, there should be opportunity for the potential candidate to meet those with whom the person would be working;

a need for increased consultation, especially with lay people.

3.4 The suggestions made in relation to *suffragan bishops* included:

that the diocesan bishop should, whilst retaining the right of nomination, consult much more widely within the diocese;

that there should be more formal consultation with the leading clergy and laity of the diocese;

that a new system involving some kind of appointing group should be established.

3.5 In relation to *deans, provosts and residentiary canons* the suggestions made included:

that the diocesan bishop should have the decisive say in the appointment of the dean of his Cathedral;

that a 'senior appointments commission' should make the choice, or that the appointment should be made by the Vacancy in See Committee, or by some 'appointing group';

that advertising and clearer job descriptions should be used;

that the appointing process should take full account of the need for the chapter and the individual to exercise a collaborative ministry;

that there was a need for appropriate methods of appraisal for people in post;

that the chapter should work together with the diocesan bishop on the job description;

that residentiary canons should no longer be regarded as senior church appointments.

3.6   The suggestions offered in relation to *archdeacons* included:

that as the 'eye of the bishop' his appointment should continue to be made by the diocesan bishop;

that the bishop should however consult more widely before making the appointment;

that some kind of 'appointments committee' should be set up to investigate the needs, to draft a job description, and to suggest possible candidates;

that there should be a balance in appointments between those drawn from outside the diocese and those appointed from within it.

3.7   We have confined ourselves in this chapter to highlighting the main points, relevant to our terms of reference, put to us in the letters we received. They reflect the suggestions made to us and should not be taken as the views of the Working Party itself. We are greatly indebted to all those who wrote to us with their comments and suggestions. Our recommendations in Chapter 6 flow from our consideration of the ideas and concerns put to us, as well as of the other material we received and from our own deliberations.

4

THE CASE FOR CHANGE

4.1   In this chapter, we consider the case for changing the present system, or rather systems, of appointment to senior clerical posts in the Church of England. We set out why we think change is necessary; the broad limits within which we consider that change should occur; and the principles which guide our subsequent recommendations.

Reasons for Change

4.2   A considerable alteration in the method of appointment to the most senior posts in the Church of England occurred in 1976 with the introduction of the present arrangements for appointing archbishops and diocesan bishops. For many years previously the Crown had made these appointments solely on the recommendation of the Prime Minister and although informal consultations were undertaken by the Prime Minister's office before advice was put to the Sovereign, the Church itself was not formally part of the appointing process (but see para. 5.12 below).

4.3   In 1976 the then Prime Minister, Mr James Callaghan, acknowledged in a statement in Parliament that the Church should have a greater say in the choice of its leaders. He announced that the Church would set up what became the Crown Appointments Commission to submit two names for consideration by the Prime Minister, from which the Prime Minister would make his recommendation to the Sovereign. The texts of the statement and of the General Synod motion to which it was a response are reproduced in Appendix V.

4.4   The current arrangement does not go as far as some people wish. The Crown's right to appoint remains intact. While the Church, through the medium of the Crown Appointments Commission, makes its two nominations, the Prime Minister submits one name which the Sovereign approves. Nevertheless the move to the present procedure represented a significant shift, giving the Church a greater say in appointments to these posts. Many saw it as a first step in a continuing process of reform of appointment procedures.

4.5 In parallel with this change in the arrangements for the appointment of archbishops and diocesan bishops in the Church, there has been a substantial change over the last five years in the way in which parochial appointments are made. Although the Patronage (Benefices) Measure 1986 did not sweep away the system of ecclesiastical patronage, it substantially altered the way that system operates by requiring for example participation by parochial church councils (PCCs) in the filling of vacancies. Both bishops and PCC representatives were given an effective right of veto over prospective incumbents suggested by patrons. It is also increasingly the practice for parochial posts to be advertised and for interviews to be held before appointments are made.

4.6 However, the procedures for appointment to other posts in the Church have remained largely unchanged for many years. As indicated in Appendix I, the setting up of our own Working Party is itself evidence of a desire to subject these procedures to a scrutiny similar to that which has been applied to the methods of appointment to other posts in the Church. Our proposals are to be seen as part of an evolutionary process of change which has gradually given the Church a greater say in its own appointments and government.

4.7 The case for change in the methods of appointment to the posts within our remit does not rest on administrative neatness. It flows from the understanding of theological and ecclesiological issues which we have set out in Chapter 2; and from our concept of the role and mission of the Church at this point in her life. It may serve to highlight that concept if we first say something about the context in which senior appointments are made in the public and private sectors. We then set out the context in which similar appointments are made in the Church.

Senior Appointments in the Public and Private Sectors

4.8   All appointments systems share the common goal of seeking to ensure that they identify the person best suited to the job in question. How they achieve that goal varies considerably, however. In public life, many if not all posts which are at the disposal of the State – such as the most senior posts in the judiciary, regius professorships, lords lieutenancies, chairmanships of publicly owned industries or other national bodies – are never advertised. Soundings are taken, a name emerges, but individuals are not given the opportunity to apply for the vacancy. By contrast, in the employed public sector – such as in education – practically all posts are advertised.

4.9   Private sector practice varies. At the senior levels, there is little public or formal advertising of posts, partly because of the perceived strength of the succession planning arrangements which most large companies operate. The first building blocks in ensuring successful succession planning are sound appraisal systems and individual career planning.

4.10   Even good succession planning will not always produce the right candidate, and it is increasingly common for large organisations to use Executive Search Consultants to help fill senior posts when that happens. The best and most reputable of these organisations begin their work by establishing that the client has thoroughly defined the role of, and the task required in, the vacant post and the kind of person best able to fulfil them. This is in some respects analogous to some parts of the proposals for new appointing processes that we make later. However, such Consultants invariably sound out potential candidates about their interest in and availability for a particular position in order to establish whether they would be willing to be considered formally.

The Church Context

4.11   The Church's aim in relation to senior appointments is no different from that of any other organisation – to find the person best suited to the post in question. The context is different, however, in a number of respects.

4.12 The primary activity of the Church is to worship God and in so doing to demonstrate the way of Christ. Through its mission and ministry, it aims to bring all people into the fellowship of Christ. In each generation, it needs people of proven sanctity and ability to lead it. Whatever the method by which its leaders are found it must be set within the context of prayer and allow for the working of the Holy Spirit. Prayer is the primary means by which the Church collectively, and its members individually, seek God's guidance.

4.13 Within the Church the concept of vocation – of being called – is particularly important. Any attempt by an individual to seek to acquire power for power's sake is frowned on. People respond to what they hear as a call from God and the Church at large to undertake a particular role. A vocation to exercise additional responsibility within the Church is not inimical to that sense of being 'called', though such a sense of vocation must always be subject to testing. The methods of appointment in operation need to be able to articulate the corporate voice of the Church in calling someone to fill a particular post.

4.14 The posts which are the subject of our study are senior church appointments because they carry a greater responsibility within the Church for leadership, pastoral care and teaching. All people in the Church – bishops, clergy and laity – are equally members of it, and are engaged in many different varieties of ministry.

4.15 These considerations must be taken into account in designing appointment procedures for the Church. It follows from its high calling that the Church should ensure that its procedures are as effective as possible.

Assessment of the Present Procedures

4.16 The evidence which we have received (cf. para. 1.4 above) indicates that the present methods of appointment to senior posts are often inadequately understood. But it is not just that people are ill-informed about them. Judged by the comments we have received, for many the processes lack credibility, for a number of reasons:

i.   they are characterised by an unnecessary and undesirable degree of secrecy and idiosyncrasy;

ii.   consultation is more often than not unstructured in relation to posts where the bishop takes the lead in making the appointment;

iii.   the principle embodied in synodical government that representatives of all sections of the Church should be involved in key decisions is not reflected in the methods of appointment to the posts with which we are concerned. Current systems do not allow adequate lay or clerical involvement;

iv.   in the case of Crown appointments, they are open to Prime Ministerial and Civil Service influence;

v.   although widespread consultation does occur in the case of Crown appointments, it is not structured (i.e. there is no certainty that specific role holders will be consulted); nor is it guaranteed;

vi.   the processes of Crown appointments are not necessarily out of step with those now operating successfully in respect of diocesan bishops but they are invisible and cannot therefore be certainly said to be in step.

4.17   From the perspective of the clergy, the processes for making senior appointments are often seen as secretive and uncertain. This contrasts with the increasing adoption by dioceses of more open ministerial development procedures, including systems of appraisal and personal development planning for individual clergy and, often, the opportunity to apply for posts. Sector ministry posts (some of which are attached to residentiary canonries) are being advertised with increasing frequency both within dioceses and in the Church press. From the perspective of the laity, there is also a marked contrast not only with their experience in many secular walks of life but with practice in appointing clergy to posts in parishes. Due account should be taken of the fact that when the appointment of an incumbent is being considered, under the terms of the Patronage (Benefices) Measure 1986, the parochial church council is required to produce a profile of the type of person required to fill a vacancy, is free to propose advertising a post, and may be involved in interviewing candidates with a view to offering advice to the patron.

Principles for the Future

4.18   Our analysis and our evaluation of all the evidence put to us leads us to enunciate two principles which underlie our approach to the development of new methods of appointment to senior posts. These are that they must be *effective* and *open*.

We see the working out of those principles as meaning:

i.   that the processes by which appointments are made should be widely known and understood;

ii.   that they should not undermine episcopal authority, but should involve a proper degree of consultation:

with clergy and laity directly affected, including synodically elected representatives;

with the wider Church (including, where appropriate, leaders of other churches in England);

in the community, to reflect and fulfil the national role of the Church of England.

iii.   this consultation should be primarily directed at defining:

the nature, duties and responsibilities of the post to which the appointment is to be made, and

the gifts, skills and personal characteristics to be looked for in the person to be appointed;

iv.   it should also include identification of the names of individuals considered suitable for appointment;

v.   the vacancy should be made known so that names can be suggested or applications received;

vi.   the final choice of appointee should continue to rest, in the case of non-Crown appointments, with the diocesan bishop;

vii.   in each case, the method of appointment should be capable of adaptation to the post in question, be robust enough to cope with changing circumstances, and be designed to secure the best appointment possible.

4.19   As regards appointments by the Crown, we have already described what we regard as the main unsatisfactory features of the present arrangements. With the exception of the appointment of diocesan bishops, those arrangements have not been formally affected by recent changes in the Church, such as increased lay involvement and the introduction of synodical government. Moreover the Crown's right to appoint to some senior posts in the Church (e.g. when an archdeacon or provost becomes a diocesan bishop) militates against the Church's attempts to plan ahead sensibly in relation to all its senior posts.

4.20   Our consultations suggest that the Crown's involvement in senior appointments through the Sovereign's role as Supreme Governor of the Established Church is greatly valued. Indeed in the letters submitted to us, especially by some members of Cathedral Chapters, arguments were advanced for leaving matters as they are. The Crown's involvement, it is said, is a very proper reflection of the current nature of the relationship between the Established Church and the State, a relationship which should not be altered. The Church gains real advantage from the Crown's use of its freedoms. The Crown brings the advantage of a different perspective to bear, and its freedom prevents bishops from having excessive powers of appointment.

4.21   We do not wish to increase the Church's 'say' in such appointments to the point at which the Sovereign's role is excluded. We recognise also that any different view on this point would raise wider implications which would take us beyond our terms of reference. Nevertheless most of us do have serious reservations about the involvement of the State in the shape of the Prime Minister and his office in the process of appointment of suffragan bishops and deans, who unlike diocesan bishops have no entitlement to a seat in Parliament. Gone are the days when membership of the House of Commons was synonymous with being a member of the Church of England. It follows that advice on these appointments can now be tendered by a Prime Minister with no affiliations to the Church of England at all or indeed to any other Christian community. Furthermore any Prime Minister of strongly held views is in a position to influence such appointments decisively. Before making our specific recommendations on how appointments should be made in future to the different types of post within our remit, we turn to consider how this difficulty may be overcome.

5

ADVICE TO THE SOVEREIGN

5.1   Suffragan bishops and deans of cathedral churches are, as a matter of law, appointed by the Sovereign who acts on the advice of the Prime Minister, and the general understanding is that it would be constitutionally improper for the Queen not to follow that advice. The Working Party needed to know whether it would be legally possible and constitutionally proper to replace this system by one under which the appointments continue to be made by the Sovereign on advice, but with the role at present exercised by the Prime Minister transferred to the Archbishops of Canterbury and York, and if so how that could be achieved.

5.2   A supplementary question was whether provosts of cathedral churches, who are not at present appointed by the Sovereign, could also be appointed by the same arrangements if the necessary legislation was passed to transfer the power of appointment to the Sovereign.

The Legal Position

5.3   There are, of course, unwritten constitutional conventions which, on one view at any rate, are binding on those concerned, even though they may not be enforceable in the courts, and there may perhaps also be wider general principles as to what is constitutionally proper. The possible impact of those conventions is dealt with later in this chapter; the present section relates to legal rules which it is thought would be enforced by the courts in the extremely unlikely event of their being called upon to do so.

5.4   The appointment of suffragan bishops is governed by the Suffragan Bishops Acts 1534 to 1898 under which the diocesan bishop submits a petition with two names, of whom the first is his preferred candidate, although it is now accepted practice that the second must also be a genuine possibility in case, for example, the first-named person dies before the appointment is made.

Although he is not required to do so as a matter of law, the diocesan bishop in practice consults the archbishop of the province beforehand, as well as anyone else he wishes, and when the petition is sent to the Prime Minister it is accompanied by a letter from the archbishop of the province supporting both names but preferring the first. The Prime Minister has, for at least the last hundred years, advised the Sovereign to accept the first-named person (provided he is available for appointment).

5.5 The dean of every dean and chapter cathedral is appointed by the Sovereign. This has its origins in history (see paragraph 14 of Appendix III), but the constitution and statutes governing each cathedral church, made under the Cathedrals Measures 1963 and 1976, are now required to provide for the appointment of the dean by Her Majesty (1963 Measure, section 10(1)(a)). The 1963 and 1976 Measures do not apply to Christ Church, Oxford, which is not only the cathedral church of the diocese but also a constituent college of the University. There the dean is appointed by the Sovereign, by custom after consultation with the teaching staff over which it is the dean's duty to preside.

5.6 Parish church cathedrals have a provost and chapter rather than a dean and chapter. The provost is the incumbent of the benefice of which the cathedral is the parish church (see Cathedral Measure 1963, section 10(1)(b)), and in most cases he is appointed by the diocesan bishop, although there are two exceptions where the right to appoint is in other hands.

5.7 The Diocese in Europe is part of the Province of Canterbury, but its own Constitution makes provision for the appointment of its suffragan bishop and appointments with regard to its cathedral churches; the questions posed in this chapter do not apply to them. The Diocese of Sodor and Man, which now also has a cathedral, is part of the Province of York, but, as in the case of the Diocese in Europe, is not affected by these issues.

5.8 The collegiate churches of Westminster (Westminster Abbey) and Windsor (St George's Chapel, Windsor) are Royal Peculiars. Each has a dean and chapter or 'college', and in each case the dean is appointed by the Sovereign, but those appointments are outside the scope of the Working Party's terms of reference.

5.9   There are a few cases where the incumbent of a church which was formerly a peculiar, although not necessarily a Royal peculiar, has retained the title of 'Dean'; one example is the Dean of Battle, in Sussex. Except in the Channel Islands, which again have their own system of ecclesiastical law in many respects, these titles now have no real legal significance and are outside the Working Party's terms of reference.

The Present Method of Appointment and the Role of the Prime Minister

HISTORICAL DEVELOPMENT

5.10   Brief accounts of the historical development of the present method of appointment of archbishops, bishops and deans are to be found at pages 25-30 of *Crown Appointments and the Church* (the Archbishops' Commission of 1964) and on pages 30-32 of *Church and State* (the Archbishops' Commission of 1970). It is clear that, especially since the time of the Hanoverian kings, the Prime Minister's influence over the Sovereign's Church appointments developed steadily. Precisely what Queen Victoria considered her own constitutional role to be in this respect is difficult to say. However, in the case of archbishops and bishops she clearly believed she was entitled to put forward her own suggestions to the Prime Minister, and there is evidence that, at the least, she considered she had and could properly exercise a right of veto over his formal advice. Berriedale Keith in *The Constitution of England from Queen Victoria to George VI*[1] suggests that this idea of a right of veto persisted, at least in theory, to the time of George V, and as late as 1954 the Archbishop of Canterbury of the day asserted in a debate in the Church Assembly[2] that the constitutional position remained the same as under Queen Victoria and the Sovereign's power of veto still existed.

[1] (1949) vol II, pp. 450, 451.
[2] *Report of Proceedings*, November 1954, pp. 460, 461.

5.11   Nevertheless, so far as is known the present Queen receives advice from the Prime Minister in the form of the name of a single person recommended for appointment as bishop or dean, and has never refused to accept it. Indeed, it is now generally thought that she would be acting improperly if she declined to follow the Prime Minister's advice; in the case of archbishops and bishops, this view may have been helped to develop, or been reinforced, by the changes in practice described in paragraphs 5.17 and 5.18. It may be that there is informal discussion between the Sovereign and the Prime Minister, and that for this purpose the Sovereign may take informal advice from others, but presumably anything of this kind takes place before the Prime Minister tenders his formal advice.

5.12   So far as the Prime Minister's advice is concerned, Gladstone created the post of the Prime Minister's Secretary for Appointments, and the holder of that post clearly developed an important role in carrying out consultations about proposed appointments. By the mid-twentieth century the Archbishop of Canterbury was invariably consulted about appointments to diocesan bishoprics, put forward his own selection of names to the Prime Minister, and was confident that the Prime Minister would not advise the Sovereign to appoint someone to whom the Archbishop had serious objections.[3] It was also the practice of the Prime Minister's appointments secretary to consult representative clergy and laity in the diocese.

5.13   In the case of deans it is usual for the Prime Minister's appointments secretary to carry out consultations with the residentiary canons of the cathedral, the diocesan bishop, possibly the greater chapter and possibly others concerned with public and church life in the diocese, before the Prime Minister gives formal advice to the Sovereign. The Prime Minister's appointments secretary may consult the Archbishops' appointments secretary but does not invariably do so.

5.14   The Prime Minister's advice on matters of church appointments is not given on behalf of the Cabinet or the

---

[3] *Cantuar* by Edward Carpenter (1971), pp. 251-8, 361-2, 373-4, 496.
Church and State by Cyril Garbett (1954), pp. 180-203.

Government, but is the Prime Minister's personal advice to the Sovereign (see the Archbishops' Commission of 1964, p. 29). He cannot be questioned in Parliament about his advice on individual appointments (Erskine May, *Parliamentary Practice* (21st ed.), p. 288), although a recent discussion in the House of Commons on the analogous position as regards the grant of honours suggests that it may perhaps be possible to put a Parliamentary Question to the Prime Minister about his general policy in such matters (*Hansard*, House of Commons, 18 December 1990, cols. 175-8).

PROPOSALS FOR REFORM AND CHANGES IN RELATION TO ARCHBISHOPS AND DIOCESAN BISHOPS

5.15   For many years there was a good deal of disquiet about the method of making senior church appointments, and particularly those of archbishops and bishops. Two major causes of concern were that the existing procedure might involve the Sovereign receiving formal advice from a Prime Minister who was not a committed member of the Church of England and that, although there was full consultation with the Church in practice, there was no guarantee of this. A brief history of the discussion in Convocation and the Church Assembly, and the various reports on it, is to be found at pages 11-20 of the Archbishops' Commission of 1964.

5.16   As a result of the recommendations in the 1964 Howick report on Church and State, a Vacancy-in-See Committee was set up for each diocese to represent the clergy and laity of the diocese in the case of a vacancy in the diocesan see, and to prepare a statement of the needs of the diocese for submission to the Prime Minister and the Archbishop. The Archbishops also created the post of their own lay appointments secretary.

5.17   However, the recommendations in the 1970 report on Church and State produced more radical changes as regards the appointment of archbishops and diocesan bishops. After discussions between the Archbishop of Canterbury and Sir Norman Anderson, QC, (on behalf of the General Synod) on the one hand and the Prime Minister and his advisers on the other, and after consultation with the leaders of the main Opposition parties, the Prime Minister of the day (Mr Callaghan) made a statement to Parliament in July 1976 which is set out in Appendix V to this Report. The arrangement outlined there was that the Sovereign would continue to receive final advice from the Prime Minister, and the Prime Minister would retain a real element of choice, but that a shortlist of names, in order of preference if so desired, would be submitted to the Prime Minister by a body set up by the Church. The Prime Minister could then either recommend a name on the list, although not necessarily the first name, or alternatively ask the church body for a further name or names.

5.18   As part of this arrangement, a Crown Appointments Commission was also established, including four members of the diocesan Vacancy-in-See Committee for the diocese in question. The composition of the Commission is set out in the General Synod's Standing Orders and in practice it invariably submits two names, usually in order of preference, to the Prime Minister. In the years since 1977, when the new arrangements came into force, those arrangements have been followed by the Prime Minister although on one view at least the Prime Minister's acceptance of the arrangements remains voluntary and could be withdrawn (see *Episcopal Ministry* (1990), p. 223).

Questions Raised by the Working Party

5.19   In considering its task, one possibility the Working Party needed to consider was whether, so far as suffragan bishops and deans of cathedral churches are concerned, appointments should continue to be made by the Sovereign but the Archbishops of Canterbury and York, in their role as Privy Counsellors, could replace the role at present played by the Prime Minister. Thus they alone would tender formal advice to the Sovereign.

5.20   In the debate on the Report of the Moberly Commission[4] it was stated that the Commission had been advised that this was constitutionally impossible, and that the 'custom in the Constitution of the Crown being advised in these matters by the Prime

---

[4] *Report of Proceedings*, November 1952, p. 315.

Minister could not be altered'. Doubts were cast upon that in 1954[5] and therefore the Working Party decided to seek Counsel's Opinion on the constitutional issues raised by the suggestions before taking them any further.

5.21 One of the questions which needed answering was whether, and if so how, unwritten constitutional rules which are binding although not necessarily enforceable in the courts may be changed, and how new rules of that kind may be created.

5.22 Geoffrey Marshall, in his book *Constitutional Conventions* (1984), suggests that a convention may be established without any previous history of custom or usage, by agreement among the persons concerned to work in a particular way and to adopt a particular rule of conduct (p. 9), and that the constitutional position may be altered by deliberate abrogation of an existing convention or creation of a new one by agreement (p. 217). The Working Party needed advice on whether a constitutional convention in the sphere of church appointments made by the Sovereign could be changed or created by agreement between Her Majesty, the Prime Minister and the Church. In addition, could the Church for this purpose, and for the purpose of the suggestions set out in paragraph 5.19, be represented by the Archbishops and was a resolution of the General Synod supporting the proposal desirable? Further, would it be necessary (or desirable) to secure the agreement of, or at least consult, the Leaders of the main Opposition parties?

5.23 Some might argue that the 1977 arrangements for the appointment of archbishops and diocesan bishops are ones from which the Prime Minister could properly withdraw if he wished, and are thus not true conventions, so that their value as a precedent in this respect is limited. However, in 1946 the Order of the Garter ceased to be awarded on the formal advice of the Prime Minister and passed into the personal gift of the Sovereign, although it was agreed that informal consultation with the Prime Minister would continue. This followed the principle which had been established in 1902 when the Order of Merit was founded, whereby that Order was to be bestowed by the Monarch without

---

[5] *Report of Proceedings*, November 1954, pp. 457, 458.

any formal submission by the Prime Minister. The 1946 change so far as the Order of the Garter was concerned was brought about at the instigation of King George VI himself, by agreement between him and the Prime Minister of the day and after consultation with the Leader of the Opposition.[6]

5.24   In addition, the Working Party needed to know whether there was any general constitutional principle that, if the Sovereign acts on formal advice in a particular matter, that advice must come from a Minister of the Crown or, possibly, someone who can be questioned about it in Parliament. This was suggested in 1952 (see para. 5.20), and although various examples of cases where the Crown does not or need not act on formal advice are known (for example, those cited by R. W. Blackburn at [1985] J.P.L. 36), it has not been possible to find any example of a case where the Sovereign acts on formal advice from someone other than a Minister of the Crown. The position of the Lord High Commissioner, who represents the Sovereign at meetings of the General Assembly of the Church of Scotland, was thought to be an exception, but it is understood that the Secretary of State for Scotland takes soundings from the Church of Scotland as to who would be a suitable candidate; names are given to the Prime Minister who advises the Sovereign on the appointment.

5.25   Finally, two subsidiary points have been raised. One is that the Archbishops of Canterbury and York are invariably Privy Counsellors (and thus have a right of audience with the Sovereign). Would this make them an exception to any general principle of the kind outlined in para. 5.24? Secondly, although both Archbishops are of course members of the House of Lords, it is understood that Parliamentary Questions cannot be addressed to them (see Erskine May, *Parliamentary Practice*, p. 422); in view of the position as set out in para. 5.14, would this constitute an objection to the Working Party's suggestions?

Counsel's Opinion

5.26   The Working Party asked Sir David Calcutt, QC, Master of

---

[6] *The Times,* 4 December 1946; *King George VI, His Life and Reign* (1956), J. W. Wheeler-Bennett, pp. 755-760.

Magdalene College, Cambridge, and Chancellor of the Dioceses of Bristol, Exeter and in Europe, to give them an Opinion on these matters.

5.27   Sir David gave two Opinions, the first with regard to deans and provosts and the second dealing with the position of suffragan bishops. The first Opinion was in the following terms:

i.   Deans of Cathedral Churches (whom I will call 'Deans') are presently appointed by the Sovereign on the advice of the Prime Minister. I am asked to advise whether it would be legally possible and constitutionally proper to replace that system by one under which such appointments continue to be made by the Sovereign, but on the advice of the Archbishops of Canterbury and York acting jointly; and, if so, how that could be achieved.

ii.   Secondly, Provosts of Cathedral Churches are, generally speaking, presently appointed by Diocesan Bishops. I am asked to advise whether it would be legally possible and constitutionally proper for them to be appointed, for the future, in the manner proposed for Deans.

iii.   This Opinion is in no way concerned with the desirability of such changes as have been suggested, but simply with legality and constitutional propriety.

iv.   In my opinion, although the matter cannot be wholly free from doubt, there is no reason why, provided there is appropriate agreement (which I consider in para. xix), the changes which have been suggested should not be made.

v.   Much of the public discussion which has taken place in the past has related to the appointment of Bishops rather than to Deans and Provosts;[1] and, while there are distinctions which may need to be drawn, much of the discussion which has taken place is relevant to the matters now under consideration.

vi.   The history relating to such appointments has already been set out extensively, and it seems to me that no useful purpose would be served by now repeating that exposition. There appears to be no doubt that there was a time when appointments were made by the Sovereign personally, on such advice as he or she saw fit to take. Significant changes occurred in the eighteenth century. Queen Victoria introduced certain idiosyncratic practices. Although today the Sovereign personally exercises rights of ecclesiastical patronage in certain exceptional cases, she does not exercise it personally in the case of Deans.

vii.   Before a name is formally submitted to the Sovereign, a wide process of consultation takes place; but, at the end of the day, the 'advice' takes the form of a nomination which, subject to any right of veto, the Sovereign accepts.

viii.   Is it now possible, in law and with constitutional propriety, to replace that system in the manner proposed? I have no doubt that it could not be changed in the absence of appropriate agreement, and particularly that of the Prime Minister. The prospect of legislation being enacted contrary to the wishes of the Prime Minister does not seem to me to be a reality.

ix.   It is not for me, perhaps, to speculate whether the Prime Minister would be likely to consent, even if in a position to do so, to the proposed changes, but there are obviously a number of matters which would be likely to concern him. It may be seen as an unwarranted diminution of the powers of the Crown and of his office. It may be seen as an undesirable weakening of the bonds of Church and State. He would, I imagine, need to be persuaded that the proposed changes would be likely to result in an overall improvement; and, having regard to the existing system of wide consultation before the formal submission of a name, this might not be readily apparent. He would also, I imagine, need to be persuaded that the changes had sufficiently wide acceptance that any call for further changes would be unlikely within a reasonable period of time. These are plainly only some of the matters which might exercise his mind.

x.   But, assuming that the proposed changes would have the Prime Minister's agreement, would it be lawful and constitutionally proper for those changes to be made?

xi.   In a debate in the Church Assembly in November 1952 Bishop Mortimer of Exeter (who was a member of the Commission appointed in 1949) is recorded as having spoken in these terms:

'The Bishop of Exeter said that this particular proposal had a charming simplicity about it but it was not so simple as to have escaped the attention of the Commission. It was before them, but the expert advice they received made it clear in the first instance

that any proposal like this was impracticable in the sense of being constitutionally impossible. They might have been wrongly informed, but they went to the highest authority that they could and they were advised that this custom in the Constitution of the Crown being advised in these matters by the Prime Minister could not be altered.'²

That view has since been questioned; and I have been unable to trace support for the advice reportedly given.

xii. In June 1976 the Prime Minister, in a written Parliamentary Answer, made a statement in these terms:

'The Sovereign, who is herself the Supreme Governor of the established Church, appoints Archbishops and Diocesan Bishops on the advice of the Prime Minister of the day .... There are, in my view, cogent reasons why the State cannot divest itself from a concern with these appointments of the established Church. The Sovereign must be able to look for advice on a matter of this kind and that must mean, for a constitutional Sovereign, advice from Ministers. The Archbishops and some of the Bishops sit by right in the House of Lords, and their nomination must therefore remain a matter for the Prime Minister's concern ...'

Deans and Provosts do not sit by right in the House of Lords, so, at least to that extent, their nomination may not be a matter for the Prime Minister's concern. But is the nomination of a Dean nevertheless a matter on which the Sovereign must be able to look for advice; and, if so, must that advice come from a Minister?

xiii. I would not doubt that the Sovereign must be able to look for advice on the appointment of Deans; and, indeed it is suggested that that advice would come from the Archbishops acting jointly. But the Archbishops, though Privy Counsellors, are not Ministers. Is this a bar to them giving, and the Sovereign receiving, the requisite 'advice' in the case of the appointment of Deans?

xiv. The matter cannot, in my view, be wholly free from doubt. But it seems to me that Ministerial responsibility to Parliament lies at the heart of this matter. I have no doubt that there are some powers, exercised by the Prime Minister, of which (in the absence of statutory enactment) he could not lawfully divest himself; he could probably not divest himself of any power for the exercise of which Ministers are answerable to Parliament. But he is probably *not answerable to Parliament for the advice given on the exercise of ecclesiastical patronage;³ his responsibility is personal. If that is so, then it is difficult to see why he should be prevented from divesting himself of the right to advise in the case of Deans.*

xv.   *A consideration of certain aspects of the grant of honours may be helpful. Two developments have occurred in recent years which are of relevance. First, George VI re-asserted the personal right of the Sovereign to confer certain honours. This change was effected simply by agreement between the Prime Minister and King George VI.⁴ It is, to my mind, an indication that a change of this kind can, both lawfully and constitutionally, be made by agreement.*

xvi.   *Secondly, the Public Honours Scrutiny Committee has recently had its role more closely defined, and it has been suggested that in the event of an adverse report from the PHSC, the Sovereign may have more than a nominal role to play.⁵ This finds an echo, in the field of ecclesiastical patronage, in relation to the right of the Sovereign to veto the advice tendered by the Prime Minister, which was being asserted by the then Archbishop of Canterbury as recently as 1954.⁶ If there is indeed still a right of veto, this must at least cast some doubt on the constitutional obligation of the Sovereign to accept the advice of the Prime Minister.*

xvii.   *The point has been raised, in general terms, about changing constitutional conventions. In my opinion, if a constitutional convention can be created by agreement, it can be similarly changed by agreement.*

xviii.   *For these reasons it is my opinion, although the matter cannot be wholly free from doubt, that there is no reason why, provided there is an appropriate agreement, the changes which have been proposed should not be made.*

xix.   *I now turn to consider how the changes might be effected in practice. It seems to me that the consent of the Sovereign, the Prime Minister and the Archbishops would be an essential pre-requisite. In practice, consent would need to be even more widely achieved. Not only would I regard it as important that there should be consent of the Cabinet, but also of all the leading parties represented in Parliament. It would also need the consent of the*

Church, which could, no doubt, be expressed by means of a resolution of the General Synod. It would then, I believe, be open to the Prime Minister to make a statement in Parliament, as was done by Mr Callaghan in June 1976.

xx. Legislation would be an alternative, but probably an unnecessary and potentially complicated alternative.

xxi. There could, of course, be no guarantee that the changes would not subsequently be reversed, but I would have thought that this would, in practice, be highly unlikely.

xxii. So far as Provosts are concerned, I can see no reason why appropriate legislation should not be enacted. If there were agreement to the proposed changes regarding Deans, it seems likely that there would also be general support for the necessary legislation to effect the change regarding Provosts. In my view this should not raise any additional legal or constitutional difficulties.

DAVID CALCUTT QC
Lamb Building, Temple, EC4
25 July 1991

References

1 *Reports of the Commission appointed by the Church Assembly (1952), the Commission appointed by the Archbishops of Canterbury and York (1964) and the Commission appointed by the Church Assembly (1970).*

2 *Report of a debate in the Church Assembly on Crown Appointments on 13 November 1952, p. 315.*

3 *Erskine May, Parliamentary Practice, 21 edition (1989), p. 288, note 8; and Hansard, House of Commons, 18 December 1990, cols. 175-8.*

4 *J.W. Wheeler-Bennett, King George VI, His Life and Reign (1958), London, pp. 756-757.*

5 *Michael De-la-Noy, The Honours System, (1985), London: Allison & Busby, pp. 142ff.*

6 *Report of a debate in the Church Assembly on Appointment of Bishops and Deans on 17 and 18 November 1954, p. 461.*

5.28 The second Opinion dealt with the position of suffragan bishops and was in the following terms :

i. In July 1991 I advised whether it would be legally possible and constitutionally proper for Deans and Provosts of Cathedral

Churches to be appointed on the advice of the Archbishops of Canterbury and York acting jointly. I am now asked to advise whether the Opinion which I then expressed would be equally applicable to the appointment of suffragan bishops.

ii.   Suffragan bishops are presently appointed under the Suffragan Bishops Acts, 1534 to 1898. I am instructed that the diocesan bishop submits a petition with two names, of whom the first is his preferred candidate, although the second must also be a genuine possibility. Although he is not required to do so as a matter of law, the diocesan bishop in practice consults the Archbishop of the Province beforehand, as well as anyone else he wishes, and when the petition is sent to the Prime Minister it is accompanied by a letter from the Archbishop supporting both names but preferring the first. The Prime Minister invariably advises the Sovereign to accept the first-named person (provided he is available for appointment).

iii.   In my opinion, although the matter cannot be wholly free from doubt, there is no reason why, provided there is appropriate agreement, the changes which have been suggested should not also be made in relation to suffragan bishops.

iv.   It is my opinion there could be no change of the kind contemplated in the absence of appropriate agreement. It seems to me that the consent of the Sovereign, the Prime Minister and the Archbishops would be an essential pre-requisite; and (as I set out in para. xix of my earlier Opinion) in practice consent would need to be even more widely achieved. The consent of the Church would need to include, in particular, the consent of the diocesan bishops collectively.

David Calcutt QC
Lamb Building, Temple, EC4
7 October 1991

Conclusions of the Working Party

5.29   We have considered Counsel's Opinion with the greatest care and interest. As we make clear earlier in this Chapter the question is not a new one for the Church; to date the view has been that, for constitutional reasons, no change could be made. Counsel now advises that, though the matter cannot be wholly free from doubt, it would be possible, subject to appropriate agreement, for the Sovereign to receive advice in the matter of the appointment of suffragan bishops and deans of cathedrals from the Archbishop of Canterbury and the Archbishop of York.

5.30   To avoid all doubt we emphasise our united desire to retain the Sovereign's role in the appointments of suffragan bishops and deans. What we are addressing here is the route by which advice on such appointments is tendered to the Sovereign, and not the subsequent appointment as such. What concerns us is the part at present played in this process by the Prime Minister of the day and his or her office.

5.31   In Chapter 6 we set out our proposals for the prior process of consultation which we recommend should take place before a suffragan bishop or dean is appointed. We believe the ultimate appointment should continue to be made by the Sovereign. We take the view however that advice to the Sovereign should in future be tendered by the Archbishop of the Province concerned. We accordingly recommend that the appropriate agreements to enable this to be possible should be sought.

5.32   While it is not our direct concern we are clear that, as in the case of the establishment of the Crown Appointments Commission, the Prime Minister of the day will doubtless feel it necessary to undertake consultations not least with the leaders of the other political parties in Parliament before any change in the existing arrangements is made. In a country such as ours with no written constitution it is only by proceeding step by step in this way that new conventions are established. It is not for us either to advise or to judge how these consultations should be undertaken, and we merely content ourselves with establishing our understanding that they would be essential preliminaries to any change which, if it came about, would doubtless be announced to Parliament in much the same way as was the decision to establish what became the Crown Appointments Commission.

6

PROPOSALS FOR CHANGE

6.1   The previous Chapters set out the reasons why we believe it right to recommend some changes in the methods of appointment and the principles upon which those changes should be based. In this Chapter we set out in detail the changes we recommend, which we believe will help to achieve a far wider degree of confidence among members of the Church generally, both clerical and lay. We hope that the effect of our recommendations will be monitored and that they will be reviewed after an appropriate period of time.

Suffragan Bishops

6.2   Under the law presently governing the appointment of suffragan bishops (see para. 5.4), the diocesan bishop is not required to undertake any prior consultation in deciding upon the two names to recommend to the Crown for appointment. In practice diocesan bishops do consult. The practice is not however formalised or visible. A consistent thread running through the letters we received was that there should be an acknowledged procedure which had built into it opportunity for wide consultations to take place.

6.3   We share the view expressed in the Report of the Archbishops' Group on the Episcopate (*Episcopal Ministry*: GS 944) that 'the diocesan bishop should continue to have the decisive say in the choice of suffragans, for they are in law his commissaries' (para. 454). We have considered carefully ways in which formal procedures might be introduced which retained the decisive say of the diocesan bishop and which ensured that appropriate consultation took place. One option we considered was to look towards the Crown Appointments Commission for the formulation of recommendations for the appointment also of suffragan bishops. We do not think that this would be appropriate or that it would be practicable.

6.4   It would not in our view be appropriate because the proper balance between national, state and diocesan interests and concerns in the appointment of suffragan bishops, and indeed in the role of a suffragan bishop, is different from that which is reflected in the constitution, procedures and role of the Crown Appointments Commission in formulating and making recommendations for the appointment of archbishops and diocesan bishops. As we have said we believe that the diocesan bishop should continue to have the decisive say in the appointment of suffragan bishops. For this reason too we believe it would be inappropriate for the Crown Appointments Commission to make recommendations also for the appointment of suffragan bishops. Nor do we believe it would be practicable, since the members of the Commission particularly the central members – are very fully committed already in discharging their present role and it would be unwise to seek to add to the Commission's existing responsibilities.

6.5   We believe that any new procedure for the appointment of suffragan bishops should be based within the diocese concerned, but that it should nevertheless also reflect the proper interest and concerns of the Church nationally. We propose that as soon as it is known that an appointment is to be considered an Appointing Group should be established within the diocese with the following membership:

Chairman:

The diocesan bishop

Members:

An archdeacon from the diocese

A rural dean from the diocese

A lay chairman of one of the deaneries in the diocese

One lay person from within the diocese appointed by the diocesan bishop

Up to two other people (clerical or lay) appointed by the diocesan bishop to represent the wider national and ecumenical interests

One person appointed by the Standing Committee of the General Synod.

6.6 The archdeacon, rural dean and lay chairman of the deanery synod who are to serve as members of the Appointing Group should be elected by and from their respective number within the diocese. In the case however of dioceses where there have been established Area Schemes under the Dioceses Measure 1978 they should be elected by and from those serving within the Area concerned.

6.7 Up to three members of the Appointing Group would therefore be appointed by the diocesan bishop. One would be a lay person from public life within the diocese. He would also appoint up to two people to represent the wider national and ecumenical interests. The Standing Committee of the General Synod would make one appointment to the Group. In making its appointment the Standing Committee should seek to achieve a clerical/lay balance within the Group. We believe that the composition of a group in the way set out above draws an appropriate balance between the diocesan and national interest and concern in the appointment of suffragan bishops and, taken together with the provisions set out below, also leaves the diocesan bishop, who would be chairman of the Group, with the decisive voice in the choice of names.

6.8 The role of the Appointing Group would be to have overall responsibility for considering the nature of the ministry expected of the person to be appointed, to consult widely within the community (see para. 6.26 below and Appendix VI), to approve a job description, to search out potential candidates and finally to recommend with the concurrence of the diocesan bishop the names of three people who would be suitable for appointment. The diocesan bishop, provided he had established that his first choice was available for appointment (cf. paras. 13 and 14 of Appendix II), would draw up a Petition to the Sovereign citing the two preferred names in order of preference. He would send this Petition, together with a supporting letter to the Archbishop of the Province indicating the preferred name. The Archbishop of the Province, as a member of the Privy Council, would then communicate the contents of the diocesan bishop's Petition to the Sovereign and indicate the preferred name for approval.

6.9   We comment in more detail in paras. 6.24 to 6.39 below on the role and method of working of the Appointing Group.

Deans and Provosts of Cathedrals

6.10   Under present law (see para. 5.5) the appointment of deans rests entirely with the Crown except in the case of the cathedrals of the Diocese in Europe and the Diocese of Sodor and Man, and of Christ Church, Oxford. The Dean of Christ Church is appointed by the Sovereign, by custom after consultation (carried out by the Prime Minister's Secretary for Appointments) with the teaching staff.

6.11   The provost of a parish church cathedral becomes such by virtue of his institution and induction as incumbent of the benefice. The procedure under which he is appointed as the incumbent of the benefice of the parish church cathedral is the same as that prescribed by Patronage (Benefices) Measure 1986 for the appointment of incumbents generally. These procedures provide that the parochial church council shall appoint two representatives to act in the vacancy and may request that the vacancy is advertised. Under the Measure the two representatives may exercise a veto on a name put forward by the patron of the benefice for appointment as incumbent of the benefice. The patronage of the benefices of parish church cathedrals is in twelve cases with the diocesan bishop, and in two cases (Bradford and Sheffield) respectively with the Simeon Trustees and with, alternately, the Sheffield Church Burgesses and the Simeon Trustees.

6.12   There is, it seems to us, an anomaly of principle in these respective provisions of the present law. In the case of appointments to deaneries there is no requirement, or formal opportunity, for the Church at a national, diocesan, or local level to be involved in the process. We recognise however that in practice the Crown's advisers do indeed consult widely within the diocese (see Appendix II). In the case of the appointment of provosts there is, under the 1986 Measure, the requirement that the representatives of the parish have a formal place in the procedure.

6.13 The nature of the particular ministry of a cathedral varies. Each cathedral is the mother church of the diocese, the seat of the bishop, and in each case the diocesan bishop is Visitor. Each provides a particular and distinct contribution to the ministry of the diocese as a whole. Cathedrals have many dimensions to their ministries including:

the link with civic and city communities,

national and international responsibilities,

ministry to its own congregation, which may be substantial.

The cathedrals of England are interwoven with the historic fabric of the country. A number of cathedral foundations date from the pre-Norman Conquest period; some date from between the Conquest and the Reformation, others were renewed and re-ordered in the post-Reformation period, and fourteen parish churches were created as parish church cathedrals in the nineteenth century and also in the early part of this century.

The twentieth century has seen a renewal in the importance of cathedrals as they develop a multilateral ministry. The expectations demanded of both deans and provosts now cover areas of management as well as collegiality and spiritual leadership, because of the enormous interest of tourists and pilgrims, the expansion of visitors and schools programmes, and the use of cathedrals as centres of music and drama. Many cathedrals are major national shrines and have complex programmes of repair and maintenance. Some cathedrals have educational foundations for which they are responsible and of which the dean or provost is chairman of the governors. Cathedral tradition demands excellence in the offering of daily worship and the singing of the choral office.

All these functions of a cathedral will increase and develop in the twenty-first century and make the process of selection for deans and provosts of increasing importance.

6.14 We take the view that arrangements should be introduced under which the preliminary steps in the process leading up to the appointment of deans and provosts should be the same. The procedures should be such as to ensure that wide consultations take place within the cathedral and also within the diocese, acknowledging the contribution the cathedral has to offer to the totality of the ministry of the diocese. We believe that the procedures should reflect too the concern and interest of the Church nationally in the appointment of deans and provosts of cathedrals which form so significant a part of the Church's, and of the nation's, heritage.

6.15   We therefore propose that, as soon as it is known that an appointment is to be made of a dean or of a provost, an Appointing Group should be established within the diocese with the following membership:

The diocesan bishop

Two lay representatives of the cathedral congregation

A residentiary canon of the cathedral

A dean or provost from another diocese

A member of the diocesan house of clergy

A member of the diocesan house of laity

A nominee of the Standing Committee of the General Synod

Two lay members to represent the concerns of the wider community, local or national, appointed by the diocesan bishop.

6.16   We recommend that the Chairman of the Appointing Group should be the diocesan bishop in the case of the appointment of a provost. In the case of an appointment to a deanery we recommend that the members of the Appointing Group should be free to choose one of their members to act as chairman.

6.17   In those dean and chapter cathedrals which already have an electoral roll, the two lay representatives of the congregation would be elected by and from amongst those on that roll. In other such cathedrals equivalent means would have to be established for undertaking the election – perhaps on the basis of a roll of the congregation. In the case of parish church cathedrals the two representatives would be those appointed under the Patronage (Benefices) Measure 1986. We include a nominee of the Standing Committee of the General Synod because the management of cathedrals is also a matter for the Church nationally, for which the General Synod and Parliament has framed legislation (e.g. the Cathedrals Measure 1963, the Care of Cathedrals Measure 1990).

6.18   The residentiary canon to serve as a member of the Appointing Group would be elected by and from among the residentiary canons of the cathedral. The dean or provost would be elected by and from among the deans and provosts of all cathedrals. The member of the diocesan house of clergy and of the diocesan house of laity would be elected by and from amongst their respective members.

6.19   The role of the Appointing Group would be to have overall responsibility for considering the nature of the ministry expected of the person to be appointed, to consult widely within the community (see para. 6.26 below and Appendix VI), to approve a job description, and to search out potential candidates.

6.20   i.   In the case of the appointment of a dean the Group would recommend, with the concurrence of the diocesan bishop, two names in order of preference;

ii.   in the case of the appointment of a provost the Group would recommend, with the concurrence of the diocesan bishop, three names.

In both cases we recommend that before the appointment was offered to any candidate the person concerned should meet the bishop and the cathedral chapter and other senior colleagues with whom a close working relationship would be necessary.

6.21   Our recommendations in relation to the appointing process up to this point assume that provosts and deans will be treated on a similar basis. Some would go further and argue that provosts, like deans, should be appointed by the Crown. There is an argument for convergence but we do not recommend this, for we recognise that at present the relationship between provost and chapter is significantly different from that between dean and chapter. Moreover such a move would take away an existing right of appointment of diocesan bishops, a step which is inconsistent with the view we have taken throughout the report on his role in making appointments. It would also require legislation. However, we recognise that the work of the Archbishops' Commission on Cathedrals may well have a bearing on this issue.

6.22   We therefore propose that once the Appointing Group had made its recommendations:

i.   In the case of candidates for a deanery the diocesan bishop would forward to the Archbishop of the Province the names of the two people in the order of preference that the Appointing Group has recommended with the concurrence of the diocesan bishop. The Archbishop of the Province, as a member of the Privy Council, would then submit a recommendation to the Sovereign of the preferred name put to him by the bishop;

ii.   in the case of candidates for any of the twelve provostships in the gift of diocesan bishops, the diocesan bishop, subject to the rights of the parish representatives under the Patronage (Benefices) Measure 1986, would appoint one of the three named persons, provided that person was available for appointment.

6.23   The patrons of the parish church cathedrals of Bradford and Sheffield are, as we have reported, respectively the Simeon Trustees, and the Sheffield Church Burgesses and the Simeon Trustees alternately. We commend the consultation procedures we have set out as ones that we hope the respective Trustees will also be ready to adopt in large measure before presenting a prospective incumbent to the diocesan bishop. As patrons of parish church cathedrals these Trustees must already exercise their patronage under the provisions of the Patronage (Benefices) Measure 1986. We do not suggest any amendment in ecclesiastical law to require them to adopt the procedures we have proposed: we hope however that they will be ready to do so.

The Process and the Role of the Appointing Groups

6.24   Underlying the proposals we have made is the importance we attach to the need for acknowledged and visible procedures which formally require that 'the Church' is consulted in the process leading up to the appointment of suffragan bishops, deans and provosts. That process of consultation also, *a priori*, requires that 'the Church' reaches a view about the nature of the task expected of the person to be appointed, the preparation of a job description, and an assessment of the kind of gifts to look for in candidates to be considered.

6.25   The total process will therefore include the following:

an exploration of the nature, emphasis and requirements in the next phase of the particular ministry; and a consideration of the characteristics sought in the person to be appointed;

consultation in the Church and the community directed at the same issues;

the preparation of a job description;

the seeking of potential candidates;

the preparation of a long list, and of a short list, of candidates;

the selection of the names to be recommended to the diocesan bishop.

6.26   The Groups would be serviced by a secretary appointed by the diocesan bishop who would have in mind that he or she should be a person of ability, perhaps with a personnel background, and certainly with an evident commitment to the Church and to the diocese concerned. He or she, with the authority of the diocesan bishop, would consult widely within the diocese, and with members of the Appointing Group. We attach as Appendix VI some outline guidelines which he or she might find helpful about the range of consultations to be undertaken.

6.27   The Archbishops' Secretary for Appointments, as Secretary to the Crown Appointments Commission, has considerable experience in the preparation of background papers appropriate for the role we have envisaged for the Appointing Groups. The knowledge he has, by virtue of his office, of people recommended for preferment will be an important resource on which the Appointing Groups should draw, particularly in the early stages of their work. The Groups will, we envisage, invite him to at least one of their meetings.

6.28 We turn now to consider two particular points arising from the evidence to us about the procedure to be adopted by the Appointing Groups in identifying potential candidates and in considering the final recommendations it should make – whether to publicise the vacancy and whether to meet shortlisted candidates before settling its final recommendations.

PUBLICISING OF VACANCIES

6.29 The Patronage (Benefices) Measure 1986 provides opportunity for the parochial church council to request that a vacancy in a benefice should be advertised. It is not unusual for vacancies for sector ministry to be advertised. Vacancies for minor canonries are frequently advertised and vacancies for residentiary canonries, when linked with a diocesan post, are often also advertised. 'Advertise' in this context would generally include the church press, and, on occasion, some of the national and regional newspapers.

6.30 Some of us take the view that the Church is not ready to move in the direction of advertising vacancies for suffragan bishops, deans and provosts. On that view, the developing processes in dioceses of schemes for appraisal and assessment of clergy (which are designed as an aid towards the development of the appropriate gifts and skills in ministry of individuals) will prove a better way to identify potential candidates for these posts. All ministry in the church is a vocation – a response to a call. Others of us, however, take the view that these posts should be advertised in the interests of openness, and so that those who may themselves feel a vocation to the role can have an opportunity to have that calling tested.

6.31 As a Working Party we see advantage and importance in making it known that the filling of a particular vacancy is to be considered (cf. para. 4.18 v. above). It does not follow from that, however, that the Appointing Group need place advertisements in local and national newspapers. The fact that there is a vacancy might be made known in more informal ways.

6.32 We do not, in these circumstances, recommend that formal advertising of these vacancies should be mandatory. We see value, however, in the Appointing Group finding at least some means (through the Diocesan Newsletter, the Clergy Appointments Adviser's vacancy list, and/or through other means) of making it known that a particular vacancy is to be considered. Moreover most of us feel there should be opportunity for applications to be made. In this way those who may feel a vocation for the particular vacancy would be able to put themselves forward. It would also enable others to bring to the attention of the Appointing Group persons they believe should be considered for appointment. The proper role of the Group is to search out the best person for the particular post: it should therefore be open to any suggestions received. We leave it as a matter for the Appointing Group to decide how it might most appropriately invite such suggestions.

6.33 One consideration the Group would need to bear in mind if it chose to advertise a vacancy formally and invite applications would be whether it could then be free also to consider candidates who had not submitted an application for the post and who would feel it inappropriate to do so. The Group's decision will have implications also on the question of the Group meeting potential candidates before making its recommendations. To this matter we now turn.

MEETING CANDIDATES

6.34 We also considered whether the Appointing Group should meet the shortlisted candidates before reaching its final view about the names it should recommend.

6.35 Some of us take the view that it is very difficult for any Appointing Group properly to consider the candidates it has shortlisted without having met those on the shortlist. References will have been taken up, not least from the diocesan bishops of the candidates concerned. But, on this view, it remains very difficult for an Appointing Group to make final recommendations for the appointment without having met the candidates. This is particularly the case where none, or not all, of the members of the Appointing Group have any previous knowledge of the shortlisted candidates.

6.36   Others of us are concerned that some good candidates for the appointment might not be willing to be interviewed (as some might not contemplate responding to an advertisement of the vacancy). Nor do interviews necessarily guarantee that a better appointment is made. There are also questions of confidentiality and of the possibility of raising expectations and the damage that can be caused when these are not met.

6.37   We believe that it should be for the Appointing Group to choose whether to interview shortlisted candidates formally, or to meet them on some kind of informal basis, but should it choose, with the concurrence of the diocesan bishop, to do either then that opportunity should be offered to each of the shortlisted candidates.

6.38   There are practical implications for the Appointing Group in the decisions it makes about advertising and about interviewing. There is the cost of administering a selection process which includes advertising and interviewing (though we do not believe that this should be the governing factor) and the number of times that the Group will need to meet. The decisions on these issues will impinge also on the question of the length of time that the particular office might remain vacant.

Archdeacons

6.39   The nature of the ministry of an archdeacon varies from diocese to diocese. Much depends, for instance, on the role of the suffragan bishop, or the area bishop in those dioceses where there are established Area Schemes. There are, however, three principal features to the work prescribed for archdeacons in canon law.

6.40   An archdeacon is responsible for assisting the bishop 'in his pastoral care and office, and particularly he shall see that all such as hold any ecclesiastical office ... perform their duties with diligence, and he shall bring to the bishop's attention what calls for correction or merits praise' (Canon C 22). The archdeacon is required to hold a yearly visitation, unless he is inhibited by the bishop, who may wish to conduct a visitation himself. He has therefore a particular relationship with the laity through his contacts with churchwardens. He is expected, as a major feature of his visitation, to enquire into the state of all the churches and churchyards in the archdeaconry, and their appurtenances. The archdeacon is responsible for inducting an incumbent into the temporalities of his benefice.

6.41 The archdeacon has therefore particular responsibilities relating to the material and temporal resources of the Church, which inevitably involve him in situations of tension and conflict. This is particularly true in the present era, when the pressure on these resources is acute. He requires prayerfulness, patience, sensitivity, clarity of thought and vision, resourcefulness, resolution of purpose, and integrity, in dealing with these situations and achieving their resolution.

6.42 In the discharge of his ministry the archdeacon is primarily the bishop's representative and officer – his 'eyes and ears'. We believe it right therefore that he should continue to be appointed by the diocesan bishop. As in the case of his nomination of a suffragan bishop, there is presently no requirement that the diocesan bishop shall undertake consultations before appointing an archdeacon. In practice most diocesan bishops do consult (see Appendix II). We believe that that practice should be developed into an acknowledged and visible process. We believe that the appropriate means would be the adoption by the House of Bishops of an agreed procedure under which diocesan bishops would undertake to consult within the diocese.

6.43 Such a procedure would include provision that:

i. all suffragan bishops, area bishops, archdeacons, the chairmen of the diocesan house of clergy and of the diocesan house of laity, rural deans and lay chairmen of deanery synods should first be consulted in general terms about their views as to the nature, emphasis and requirements of the next phase of the particular ministry and of the characteristics to be sought of the person to be appointed. If the archdeaconry is to be held together with a residential canonry it is essential that the dean or provost concerned should also be consulted;

ii.   a synopsis of the responses received and a draft job description should be prepared for comment by the bishop's council;

iii.   the diocesan bishop, having considered the responses received and the comments of his bishop's council, would settle the nature of the ministry to be undertaken, and the kind of qualities that should be looked for in any candidates and the job description;

iv.   these details should be sent to those referred to in i. above by the diocesan bishop together with an invitation to those concerned to suggest to him, in complete confidence, names for consideration;

v.   the diocesan bishop would himself be in touch with the Archbishops' Secretary for Appointments and with others, including other diocesan bishops, about possible names for consideration;

vi.   the diocesan bishop would consider all names put to him before making his final choice.

In designing the procedures the diocesan bishop might wish to take account of what we have said in paras. 6.29 to 6.38 about publicising the vacancy and about interviewing.

6.44   We believe a procedure of this kind agreed by the House of Bishops would ensure that appropriate consultations take place, would make it known that such would take place, and would be sensitive to the fact that an archdeacon is primarily a representative of and officer of the diocesan bishop.

6.45   We considered whether to recommend that the diocesan bishop, in implementing the procedure we have outlined, should establish a formally designated Group to work with him. We decided not to make such a formal recommendation. We believe that the procedure we have set out, adopted formally by the

House of Bishops as a Code of Practice, would be sufficient and appropriate.

Residentiary Canons

6.46   We have set out in Appendix II the present provisions governing the appointment of residentiary canons. Each cathedral is in law an independent corporate body governed under the provisions made in its statutes. The provisions made in the statutes vary in both substance, detail and scope from one cathedral to another. For example, some are freehold and some are leasehold.

6.47   A number of issues were raised with us, or came to the fore, in the course of our discussions about the method of appointment of the residentiary canons. Was the present process of appointment one which enabled and encouraged the development of a shared understanding within the cathedral of its corporate ministry? How should the ministry of the cathedral be seen as part of the corporate ministry of the diocese as a whole? What is, and should be, the ecclesial relationship of members of cathedral chapters and others exercising a ministry within the diocese? How is that ecclesial relationship expressed in circumstances where a residentiary canonry is held together with a diocesan appointment such as archdeacon, diocesan missioner, or diocesan director of ordinands? Is there more scope for the administration of a cathedral to be undertaken by suitably qualified lay people and, if so, how might their contribution best be reflected in the cathedral statutes?

6.48   For us to consider all these questions in detail would have taken us beyond our remit, which is to consider methods of appointment. We welcome therefore the announcement in May 1992 of the Archbishops' Commission on Cathedrals. A number of the questions we raise will, we hope, be taken into account in the course of the Commission's work. We do make, however, a number of proposals about the processes of appointment of residentiary canons which we believe will help to ensure that these issues are held to the fore in the course of the process leading up to their appointment.

6.49   We are not persuaded that there should be changes in relation to those with whom the appointments presently rest – in a number of cases this is with the Crown but in the great majority of cases it is with the diocesan bishop (cf Appendix II). But we are clear that a standard of best practice for the prior processes needs to be set by the House of Bishops which would parallel, in broad terms, the present arrangements for the appointment of incumbents, including the possibility of advertising these posts.

6.50   What we have in mind (in relation to those canonries in the gift of the diocesan bishop) is that when a vacancy arises the diocesan bishop should initiate a process under which:

i.   after discussion with the diocesan bishop, the dean (or provost) and chapter should consider and prepare for his agreement a statement setting out the needs in the post for the next phase of ministry and the kind of gifts that should be looked for in the person to be appointed. Where, however, the canonry in question is linked with a diocesan post, the diocesan bishop should take the lead in preparing this statement, but in consultation with the dean (or provost) and chapter;

ii.   in the light of i. a job description would be prepared and agreed, together with a profile of the kind of person it would be appropriate to appoint and for what tenure;

iii.   the diocesan bishop would then gather potential names for appointment, including any put forward by the dean/provost and chapter;

iv.   the diocesan bishop, having identified the person he felt it appropriate to appoint, would consult informally with the dean/provost concerned before extending an invitation to the candidate in question;

v.   before the appointment is offered to the preferred candidate, he or she would meet the bishop, and the members of the cathedral chapter and other senior colleagues with whom he or she would work.

6.51   These prior elements in the appointing process would provide opportunity for discussion and agreement about the role of each residentiary canon in relation to the corporate ministry of the cathedral itself and in relation to the role of the cathedral within the context and strategy for the ministry and mission of the diocese as a whole. They would also provide room for discussion and agreement by those concerned about the extent to which there should be scope among the cathedral's staff for the exercise, perhaps under a limited tenure, of particular special gifts – say as a theologian or as a missioner. Such discussions could, potentially, also further enable opportunities for ministry development within and between dioceses.

6.52   We believe it is important that the dean/provost and chapter and the diocesan bishop should be very fully involved in prior discussions about the appropriate kind of ministry to be exercised by a residentiary canon, and in assessing the kind of gifts therefore to be looked for in the person to be appointed. We hope that those responsible for advising on appointments to canonries in the gift of the Crown and of the Lord Chancellor will be sympathetic to those needs and operate in a similar manner.

7

IMPLEMENTATION AND COST IMPLICATIONS

Implementation

7.1 The recommendations we make in Chapter 6 concern the prior process of consultation that should take place before an appointment is made. The ultimate appointment would, however, continue to be made by the Sovereign or by the bishop. The prior processes for consultation which we recommend are capable of being implemented by agreement with those concerned. As we have said (see para. 5.31) our recommendation that advice to the Sovereign on the appointment of suffragan bishops and deans should in future be tendered by the Archbishop of the Province is again a matter capable of implementation with appropriate agreements.

Cost Implications

7.2 We have recommended that a Group of eight people should be established to consider recommendations concerning the appointment of a suffragan bishop (para. 6.5) and that a Group of ten people should consider recommendations for the appointment of a dean or a provost (para. 6.15). If the pattern of vacancies over the last five years is a reliable guide, there is likely to be a need for ten Appointing Groups each year – seven for suffragan bishops and three for deans and provosts. It would be unusual for more than one Appointing Group to be required in any diocese in any one year.

7.3 We also set out in Chapter 6 a general framework within which these Groups will work. We believe it right that each Group should decide for itself, and in its own circumstances, the way it wishes to discharge its remit (Appendix VI), including the number of times it wishes to meet. The travel etc. expenses of members will clearly have to be met by the diocese. These expenses, for a group of eight or ten people largely from within the diocese, are likely to be modest.

7.4   We have recommended (para. 6.26) that each Group should be serviced by a secretary appointed by the diocesan bishop who would undertake much of the preliminary work. He or she would incur travel and other expenses and would need access to some secretarial help. The extent of his or her expenses would depend very much on the way in which the Group decides to approach its task.

7.5   We have recommended (para. 6.27) the Archbishops' Secretary for Appointments as an important resource on which the Group and its Secretary should draw, both for his experience in the kind of role the Appointing Group would have and for his knowledge of people recommended for preferment.

7.6   The Archbishops' Appointments Secretary already undertakes a good deal of work in connection with appointments to the posts with which we are concerned (see Appendix II), but we realise that he also has to serve the Crown Appointments Commission and that he has other duties to fulfil as well. The staff for this work consist solely of the Appointments Secretary and his personal secretary. He has made it plain that in his judgement additional resources will be needed if, as we recommend, he is to be an important resource for the work of the Appointing Groups. 'Additional resources' means more staff but also accommodation and ancillary facilities for them. If the workload becomes such as to require a full-time assistant and attendant secretarial service then the costs, including the resultant overheads, could ultimately be £70,000 p.a. at current prices, although we regard that as an absolute maximum.

7.7   We find it hard to judge at this stage the extent to which he would need additional resources, for much will depend on the demands made upon his office by the Appointing Groups. That will only become clearer once our recommendations, if adopted, have been in operation for a period; and it will be important that the Appointments Secretary is continuously aware of the need to minimise expense wherever sensibly possible. For its part the

Synod will need to be mindful that in a small office a point may be reached at which adding new work can add disproportionately to costs. In this instance, that point may be at hand.

APPENDIX I

Origins, Terms of Reference, Membership, Meetings, Comments and Suggestions Invited

Origins and Terms of Reference

1. In November 1985 the General Synod debated a Report – *Crown Appointments: Report by the Standing Committee* (GS 706). Appended to that Report was *The Report of the Crown Appointments Review Group* (GS 706A) prepared by a Group comprising: the Rt Revd and Rt Honourable the Lord Blanch of Bishopthorpe, the Revd Professor Henry Chadwick, DD, FBA, KBE, and Mr O. W. H. Clark, CBE.

2. These Reports were concerned with a review of the constitution and methods of operation of the Crown Appointments Commission – in effect a review of the arrangements for the appointment of archbishops and diocesan bishops which were agreed between Church and State in 1976/77 and which had been in operation since then (cf. para. 5 of GS 706A).

3. These two Reports were the first stage in the two-stage process for the further consideration of the issue of Crown Appointments in the Church announced by the Standing Committee of the General Synod in June 1983 (cf. para. 1 of GS 706). The second stage in the process was to have been a 'broader based working party . . . to look more widely at the issue of Crown Appointments' (ibid.). The Standing Committee came, however, to the view:

> Looking at the situation now, in the light of the findings of the review of the operation of the Crown Appointments Commission, the Committee have come to feel that, while there should now be a further stage, it should have a more specific focus than they suggested in July 1983. Accordingly, they propose to set up a working party which will be concerned specifically with the methods of appointment of suffragan bishops and of deans and provosts. In both

these categories, there is (as indicated in paragraph 20) need for particular reflection of the interests of the diocesan bishop, and of the diocese as well as of the wider Church.

(quoted from para. 21 of GS 706)

4.   Accordingly, one of the motions moved, on behalf of the Standing Committee by the then Bishop of Rochester (the Rt Revd R. D. Say), in the November 1985 debate was in the following terms:

That this Synod asks the Standing Committee to proceed with the appointment of a working party to review the methods of appointment of Area and Suffragan Bishops and of Deans and Provosts as proposed in Part II of the [Standing] Committee's Report [GS 706].

5.   The Dean of Lichfield (the Very Revd J. H. Lang) moved an amendment to the terms of this motion which the General Synod accepted (*Report of Proceedings* of the General Synod for November 1985, pp. 972 *et seq*). The motion was carried in the following *amended* form:

That this Synod asks the Standing Committee to proceed with the appointment of a working party to review the methods of appointment of Area and Suffragan Bishops and of Cathedral Clergy.

6.   In the autumn of 1987 the Standing Committee extended invitations to serve on a Working Party to work to the terms of reference the General Synod had agreed.

7.   In setting up the Working Party the Standing Committee:

i.   set out that the term 'Cathedral Clergy' in the terms of the resolution passed by the General Synod should be interpreted as including deans, provosts and residentiary canons of cathedrals, but as excluding minor or honorary canons; and

ii.   asked for a comprehensive report rather than a series of separate reports on the methods of appointment to each of the offices with which we were to be concerned.

8.   At our first meeting we recognised that our terms of reference precluded us from considering also the method of appointment of archdeacons. At our request the Standing

Committee subsequently agreed to expand our terms of reference so as to enable us to do so.

Membership and Meetings

9. The membership of the Working Party was as follows:

Sir William van Straubenzee, MBE (Chairman)

Mrs Jill Dann (Vice-Chairman)

The Rt Revd C. C. Barker (until his retirement in April 1991, Suffragan Bishop of Selby)

The Provost of Birmingham (the Very Revd P. A. Berry)

The Revd Professor Henry Chadwick, DD, FBA, KBE (from November 1990 as a Consultant)

The Bishop of Chelmsford (the Rt Revd J. Waine)

The Lord Williams of Elvel (until October 1990)

The Archdeacon of Exeter (the Ven J. Richards) (from December 1988)

Mr Frank Field, MP (from March 1991)

Mr Ian Gow, MP (until July 1990)

Dr Sheila Grieve

Sir Timothy Hoare Bt

The Revd Canon Dr Trevor Park

Mr Roger Sims, MP (from March 1991)

The Revd Canon Ivor Smith-Cameron

Assessors

The Secretary-General of the General Synod (the Revd Sir Derek Pattinson until his retirement in August 1990 and Mr P. J. C. Mawer from that date)

The Legal Adviser (Mr B. J. T. Hanson)

The Archbishops' Secretary for Appointments (Mr H. J. F. McLean)

Secretary

Mr N. D. Barnett of the General Synod Office assisted, from September 1990, by Mr P. A. W. Hopkins.

10.   As will be clear, there have been a number of changes in the membership of the Working Party since our first meeting in June 1988. It was following the Standing Committee's agreement to extend our terms of reference to include consideration of the method of appointment of archdeacons that we were able to welcome the appointment of the Archdeacon of Exeter as a member of the Working Party in December 1988.

11.   Sadly, however, since our first meeting there have had to be three further changes in our membership. The first of these arises from the tragic murder of Mr Ian Gow in July 1990. He had made an enormous contribution to our discussions and we have missed him greatly as a friend and colleague. Lord Williams, on his election in the autumn of 1990 as Deputy Leader of the Labour Party in the House of Lords, very understandably felt that he could no longer continue as a member of the Working Party. We fully recognised the additional pressures upon him and we pay tribute to the contribution he too made to our work.

12.   The Standing Committee appointed Mr Roger Sims, MP and Mr Frank Field, MP to succeed Mr Gow and Lord Williams as members of the Working Party. Both were able to join us from our meeting in March 1991.

13.   We have been enormously helped by Professor Chadwick as a member of the Working Party. In the course of 1990, however, he had to let us know that, because of other major pressures on his time, he could not continue as a full member. He agreed, however, to continue as a Consultant to us. We are indebted to him.

14.   We have met on 24 occasions, including nine meetings held residentially over weekends.

Comments and Suggestions Invited

15. At an early stage in our work we wrote to each diocesan bishop, suffragan bishop, dean, provost, archdeacon and residentiary canon inviting personal and confidential comments and reflections on the methods of appointment to those offices with which we were to be concerned. We also wrote to each diocesan secretary, to the lay chairman of each diocesan synod, to the Sheffield Church Burgesses and to the Simeon Trustees as patrons of the parish church cathedrals of Bradford and Sheffield.

16. We invited corporate submissions from the Standing Committees of the House of Bishops, the House of Clergy and the House of Laity of the General Synod and from the Deans and Provosts Conference.

17. We invited submissions more widely in a letter sent to local, national and church papers. We also invited contributions from members of the General Synod.

18. Letters inviting submissions were sent out on 12 July 1988. A further letter was sent when the terms of reference were extended to include archdeacons. Some people therefore made more than one submission. We received in total 283 letters as follows:

from Diocesan Bishops	47
from Suffragan Bishops	41
from Deans/Provosts	32
from Archdeacons	39
from Residentiary Canons	51
from Diocesan Secretaries	15
from Lay Chairmen of Diocesan Houses of Laity	16
from others	42
	283

When inviting submissions we gave an assurance that all received would be treated in the strictest confidence. We are grateful to all those who wrote; we do not, however, in our Report, make any attributions of points made to us.

19. In the course of our work we also received evidence in person from a number of people:

i. The then Prime Minister (the Rt Hon. Margaret Thatcher MP) agreed that the Prime Minister's Secretary for Appointments should meet us;

ii. The Provost of Sheffield met us to assist us in our theological reflections;

iii. Professor David McClean, as Chairman of the Standing Committee of the House of Laity of the General Synod, met us to discuss the paper of evidence the Standing Committee of that House had submitted;

iv. Canon P.H. Boulton, then Chairman of the Standing Committee of the House of Clergy of the General Synod, met us to discuss the paper of evidence the Standing Committee of that House had submitted;

v. The Bishop of Sodor and Man (the Rt Revd Noel Jones) met us to discuss, as former Chaplain of the Fleet, a paper concerning processes of appointment and career planning in the Naval Chaplaincy Service;

vi. Sir Leonard Peach, Director of Personnel and Corporate Affairs for IBM, met us to discuss recruitment, appointment and appraisal practices within IBM;

vii. The First Civil Service Commissioner, Mr John Holroyd, prepared a paper for us concerning selection and appointment procedures in the Civil Service. The Chairman of the Civil Service Selection Board, Mr Julian Moore, met us to discuss this paper;

viii. The Rt Revd and Rt Hon. the Lord Blanch of Bishopthorpe, who had chaired the report on the review of the Crown Appointments Commission (GS 706A), met us and responded to a number of issues members raised with him;

ix. Canon I. Hardaker, as Clergy Appointments Adviser, met us to discuss a paper he had prepared;

x. Chancellor Sheila Cameron, as Chairman of the Archbishops' Group on the Episcopate, met with us to discuss a number of issues arising from the Group's report *Episcopal Ministry* (GS 944).

APPENDIX II

Current Processes for Making Appointments to Posts within the Working Party's Remit

1. This appendix has two purposes: to describe, first, the legal provisions that apply to each kind of appointment in the remit of the Working Party, and, second, the steps by which these appointments are made. It is based on information provided by the General Synod's Legal Adviser, the Prime Minister's Secretary for Appointments (PAS) and the Archbishops' Secretary for Appointments (AAS). The appendix includes description of the relevant elements of the work carried out by the AAS and the PAS. Their roles are not identical, for the former's task is to give advice and make recommendations to those charged with making senior appointments, whereas the latter acts as an arm of the Prime Minister's office.

In each section the opening paragraphs state the legal position and the subsequent paragraphs illustrate the practice.

This Appendix reflects current practice and was therefore written before the coming into force of the Church of England (Miscellaneous Provisions) Measure 1992 which will enable deacons to be appointed as residentiary canons. It makes no reference to future opportunities for women deacons.

Suffragan Bishops

2. The legal position is that the appointment of suffragan bishops is governed by the Suffragan Bishops Acts 1534 to 1898. (There are at present 66 suffragan bishops.) Section 1 of the 1534 Act provides that the diocesan bishop shall name and elect 'two honest and discrete spiritual persons' to the King requesting His Majesty to give one such of the said two persons as shall please His Majesty such title, name, style and dignity of bishop of one of the sees named in the Act.

3. In practice the petition is submitted for Royal approval

through the Prime Minister. For almost a hundred years the convention has been that the Prime Minister advises the Sovereign to nominate the person who is named first in the bishop's petition for appointment to the vacant see. The Sovereign then issues Letters Patent requiring the Archbishop of the Province to consecrate the nominee (if he is not already in episcopal orders) and invest him as the Bishop Suffragan of the See designated within his Province. The Suffragan Bishops Act 1898 made it lawful to nominate as a suffragan bishop a person who was already consecrated a bishop. As a consequence of these statutory provisions it is not permissible to consecrate a bishop other than to a specific see so that any form of roving episcopal commission that may be required for a particular reason can only be undertaken by a priest already in episcopal orders.

4.   The Dioceses Measure 1978 gives power to a diocesan bishop to submit a draft scheme to the Dioceses Commission for the division of the diocese into areas specifying the suffragan bishop of the diocese to whom is delegated under the authority of the diocesan (or shared with the diocesan) episcopal oversight of each area. Where a suffragan bishop has his own area under a section 11 scheme pursuant to the Dioceses Measure, he is styled 'area bishop' but, in law, he continues to be a suffragan bishop appointed in the same way as a suffragan who has no area jurisdiction.

5.   For completeness it should be noted, in addition, that (at the time of writing) there are currently three full-time stipendiary assistant bishops. Such appointments are made by a diocesan from among already consecrated bishops. They are not appointed to a particular see, nor is the appointment subject to the Sovereign's approval.

6.   When a suffragan see is vacant the diocesan bishop has considerable freedom in choosing how to proceed to fill it. For instance he is not legally bound to consult or take advice before deciding on the two names to include in the petition to the Sovereign although in practice he will consult the Archbishop of the Province, who has the duty to consecrate the preferred candidate as required of him by the Sovereign. He is not required

to consult people in his diocese, nor the AAS, although diocesan bishops invariably do both.

7.   The diocesan bishop will usually have ample notice of a vacancy, either because the suffragan's retirement date will be known or because, being close colleagues, the suffragan will have discussed his intentions with the diocesan some way ahead of the event. Sudden illness or death of a suffragan may catch a diocesan unprepared but generally he can consider what process will best meet the need in good time. He may be able to make discreet enquiries before the event, establishing, for example, how best to seek the views of his Bishop's Council about the priorities of the next suffragan episcopate and additional or alternative ways of identifying likely candidates. He may well consult the AAS at this stage. The more public steps await the public announcement of the resignation. (The timing and the processes for this are a matter for the two bishops themselves).

8.   Whether or not the AAS has been involved beforehand, he will contact the diocesan bishop as soon as he receives a formal letter from the Prime Minister's office advising him that the Sovereign has approved the resignation of the incumbent bishop. He will send him a detailed *aide-memoire* on behalf of the Provincial Archbishop which sets out the formal procedures which have to be carried out and also suggests ways in which the total process up to and including the time that the new bishop starts his ministry might be conducted.

9.   The *aide-memoire* reminds the bishop that each of the two names in the petition to the Sovereign must be a realistic candidate from the diocesan's point of view. This is a necessary precaution against the possibility of the first name falling, for whatever reason, since in that event the Crown would take up the second name.[1]

---

[1] This has been the practice for a number of years. The Cameron Report (*Episcopal Ministry*) states in footnote 22 on p. 222 that the second name is 'in a sense a sleeping partner'. That is only so to the extent that the second name will be unaware that his name has been submitted but he will be a *bona fide* candidate.

10.   The bishop, having decided how to go about choosing his suffragan, begins his work. His enquiries will range as widely as he chooses. He may very well consult members of his bishop's council and/or his diocesan synod to satisfy himself that his own view of the role and the forthcoming work corresponds with the view of the council or synod but, generally speaking, he would not discuss names with them. He may seek suggestions about names from particularly close colleagues such as members of his staff meeting, and from other knowledgeable individuals whose judgement and discretion can be trusted. He will certainly make enquiries among his brother diocesan bishops.

11.   He will almost always seek the views of the AAS, but the latter will also take the initiative and offer his services if he has not been contacted. He seeks to establish with the diocesan bishop what specific requirements there are in the vacant suffragan see, both in general but also in regard to the next episcopate. For example, he will wish to establish whether churchmanship is an important issue and if so in what direction; and he would also wish to know whether the role will have a specified geographical area to oversee or whether the role is designed round specific tasks. He will also try to establish whether there are particular challenges for the new bishop.

12.   Armed with the preliminary views of the diocesan bishop, the AAS will produce a first list of candidates for his consideration, based on material in his own files which will have been gathered through his regular and continuous searching for information, both formal and informal, about men of outstanding ability. In considering whose names to put on this list, the AAS may check some of his ideas with the bishop in whose diocese a man is currently working. The AAS will tell the Archbishop concerned the names that he has suggested and he will advise him, if he knows, on the progress of the diocesan bishop's consultations.

13.   When he has decided who his preferred candidates are, the diocesan bishop will usually discuss them with the Archbishop at this stage. Normally the diocesan will then see his preferred candidate and when he is satisfied with his own choice he will ask

the individual if he would be prepared to accept an invitation from the Sovereign were it to be made. If the man felt he would be unable to accept for any reason, the diocesan bishop would see his second choice, and so on as necessary, until a priest of his choice indicated his willingness to accept. (The second name in the final petition will not have been approached, since the diocesan only makes an approach when he expects it to be followed by an invitation to take the appointment).

14. Once the man has agreed in principle he will be invited to undergo a thorough medical examination; a report goes to the diocesan bishop and providing he is satisfied that it is right to proceed he draws up a petition, usually prepared for convenience by the Provincial Registrar, for submission to the Sovereign. A supporting letter from the Archbishop will also be prepared and the two are sent to 10 Downing Street. The Prime Minister will communicate the contents of the petition to the Sovereign, indicating the preferred name for approval.

15. The formal letter indicating the Sovereign's approval of the appointment is sent to the bishop designate from 10 Downing Street.

16. At this stage the Archbishops' Adviser on the Induction and Continuing Ministerial Education of Bishops is brought into the picture.

17. The public announcement of the new appointment is made from Downing Street, the diocesan bishop and the bishop designate having been advised of the date.

18. The final stage in the process is the consecration of the new bishop, the timing of that being determined by dates set aside in the Archbishop's calendar for the year at some much earlier date.

19. The steps of the process are identical when an area bishop is being appointed because, as indicated earlier, an area bishop is formally a suffragan, but the diocesan may consult more extensively within the area concerned and less in the rest of the diocese.

20.   Finally, it must be noted that the diocesan bishop does not divulge to others (apart from his Archbishop and the AAS) names he has recommended to the Sovereign, to respect the Crown's privacy, and also the privacy of the individuals concerned and their families.

Deans

21.   With the exception of the cathedrals for Sodor and Man and Europe which are not governed by the Cathedrals Measure 1963, that Measure provides that the constitution and statutes of each cathedral church shall provide for the appointment of any dean by the Sovereign (sec. 10(1)(a)). It should be noted additionally that the Dean of Christ Church, Oxford, is appointed through the same process (see para. 5.5).

22.   Thus the statutes of all 27 dean and chapter cathedrals provide that the dean shall be appointed by the Sovereign by Letters Patent, which in practice means that the Sovereign looks to the Prime Minister as the sole source of formal advice. The Royal Peculiars (Westminster Abbey and St George's, Windsor), being extra-provincial as well as extra-diocesan, are outside these arrangements.

23.   There are three distinct stages in the formulation of this advice. First, the PAS carries out a careful appraisal of the duties and responsibilities which will be assigned to the appointee, taking account of the opportunities and the problems of the post as well as the needs and wants which were mentioned in the consultations. He will speak to the diocesan bishop to establish the role the bishop envisages for the dean and the cathedral within the life of the Church in the diocese. He usually spends two days visiting the cathedral and talking to as many people as possible – including the canons residentiary, the greater chapter, lay staff, representatives of the congregation and relevant leaders in the local community. He will, if possible, also seek the views of the retiring dean. The consultations are designed to enable the PAS to frame a clear picture of the kind of person who might be considered for appointment. They are carried out on behalf of the Prime Minister and made in strict confidence.

24.   The second stage is the assembling of names of possible candidates, sometimes running to a very long list. This will be made up of suggestions which emerge in the course of consultations, of specific recommendations made by those in authority in relevant parts of the church itself (and especially those of the local bishop), and from the knowledge of men seen to be ready for higher preferment which is gained in the ongoing work of advising on parochial appointments and from maintaining close contact with church advisers. These will usually include the AAS, who will generally also have offered some suggestions to the bishop as a contribution to the latter's preparation for his discussion in stage one.

25.   The third and final stage is to identify from within the names assembled at stage two the most suitable available candidate for the Prime Minister to recommend for appointment by the Sovereign. This will include further consultation with church authorities at the highest level, and a considerable effort to take an objective view of the conclusions drawn from the first and second stages of the process. At the same time, Crown Prerogative in making an appointment of the Sovereign's choice on the recommendation of the Prime Minister is fully maintained.

26.   Once the Prime Minister has decided on a name the person concerned will be asked if he is willing for his name to go forward to the Sovereign for appointment. Subject to that the Prime Minister will recommend to the Sovereign that he be appointed. The Sovereign acts upon that advice.

Provosts

27.   The cathedrals which are not dean and chapter cathedrals are styled by the Cathedrals Measure 1963 as 'parish church cathedrals'. This means that, when elevated to the rank of cathedral, they retain their parish, their patron and the office of incumbent. The Cathedrals Measure stipulates that in the case of a parish church cathedral the statutes shall provide 'for the appointment as provost of the incumbent of the benefice of which the cathedral is the parish church' (sec. 10(1)(b)).

28.   Being a parish church, on a vacancy the patrons of the benefice appoint the new incumbent. This is done in the same way as the appointment to any ordinary benefice and, on appointment, the incumbent automatically becomes provost by virtue of the constitution and statutes of the cathedral.

29.   In twelve parish church cathedrals the patron is the diocesan bishop. In Bradford the patron is Simeon's Trustees and in Sheffield the alternate patrons are the Sheffield Church Burgesses and Simeon's Trustees.

30.   In the case of most provostships the AAS is directly involved, in contrast to the case of deaneries. Since provosts are beneficed clergy appointed to that extra role by the bishop, it is a matter for the patron in the first instance to decide whether he will consult and with whom; in the two cathedrals where the bishop is not the patron the diocesan bishop is normally consulted; so too, in all parish church cathedrals, are the chapter and other relevant people in the local community.

31.   Whether invited or not, the AAS will do his best to make some suggestions, since the essence of his role is to try and ensure that the needs of the Church as a whole are taken into account in the making of any senior appointment.

32.   While the patron (if he is not the bishop) is determining his preferred candidate, the bishop usually indicates to his Archbishop who the leading candidates are and his own preference, but that is not invariable since the patron is free to make his own choice of provost. The invitation to the priest to accept the benefice will be from the patron, and the invitation to accept the provostship from the bishop.

Canons Residentiary

33.   The Cathedrals Measure provides that the constitution and statutes of each cathedral shall 'provide for the appointment of canons in such manner as may be specified in the constitution and statutes' (sec. 10(1)(c)).

34.   In all cathedral constitutions, there is power to abolish or suspend a canonry for financial reasons and *ad hoc* enquiries would be needed to ascertain how many canonries remain unfilled at a given moment. The total of canonries is therefore approximate but is currently about 160.

35.   By far the majority (about 135 at present) are in the gift of the diocesan bishop but the Sovereign has rights of appointment to certain residentiary canonries in eight cathedrals, including Christ Church, Oxford, and the Lord Chancellor in three others. Additionally, the Vice-Chancellor of Cambridge University appoints one canon to Ely Cathedral, and the Dean of St Albans appoints his sub-dean, with the concurrence of the diocesan bishop in each case.

36.   The 1963 Measure also makes it possible for canons residentiary to continue in office 'for a specified term of years only, either with or without eligibility for re-appointment' (sec. 11(2)(c)). In ten cathedral constitutions power has been taken to appoint canons for a term of years. In most cases the bishop has discretion whether to make an appointment without limit of time or for a fixed term of either five, seven or ten years, usually renewable at the discretion of the bishop. There are 30 canonries capable of being leasehold.

37.   The processes for appointing a canon vary considerably from cathedral to cathedral and over time. In the case of residentiary canonries which are in the Crown's gift (including those of the Lord Chancellor), the steps taken are similar to those leading to a dean's appointment.

38.   Of those residentiary canonries in the gift of the bishop, an increasing number are used as a base for specialist ministry, often in conjunction with or on behalf of the diocese. The AAS is often asked for suggestions to fill these posts, and he must ensure that he has a clear understanding of the kind of role that is being filled at the time.

Archdeacons

39.   Both statute law and Canon Law are silent concerning the

person or body who appoints archdeacons. Watson, in the *Clergyman's Law* (1747), says 'archdeaconries are commonly given by bishops, who do therefore prefer to the same by collation. But if the archdeaconry be in the gift of a layman, the patron doth present to the bishop, who institutes in like manner as to another benefice'.

40.   As far as is known, no archdeaconries remain in private hands and they are all in the gift of the diocesan bishop. The circumstances in which the Sovereign can appoint are set out below (see Additional Appointments by the Crown). The total number of archdeaconries is 120.

41.   The steps in appointing an archdeacon are very similar to those for appointing a suffragan bishop, save that there is no expectation that the diocesan will consult his Provincial Archbishop. He may consult members of his bishop's council and it would be common to consult rural deans and deanery lay chairmen in the archdeaconry about the work to be done and perhaps about candidates within the diocese.

42.   He is, however, strongly advised to consult the AAS, and most bishops do. In any case, the AAS makes it his business to offer suggestions as soon as he sees that there is a vacancy.

43.   It has been custom and practice in many dioceses for archdeacons to be appointed from within the diocese. In this role especially, deep knowledge of the life of the Church in a diocese and the strengths and weaknesses of the clergy is held to be particularly important.

44.   At the same time, varied experiences of ministry around the Church also need to be brought to bear and the AAS will therefore more often than not draw to a diocesan bishop's attention candidates from outside the diocese to consider for appointment to an archdeaconry.

Additional Appointments by the Crown

45. Under the general law the Crown appoints to a vacant freehold benefice when the incumbent is appointed to a diocesan bishopric or the patron is the diocesan bishop and the see is vacant.

46. Thus, if the office of provost, archdeacon or canon residentiary becomes vacant by virtue of the incumbent having been appointed a diocesan bishop, the Sovereign will appoint the next provost, archdeacon or canon.

47. If the see is vacant and the office of provost becomes vacant in one of the twelve dioceses where the bishop is patron, the Sovereign will appoint the next provost.

48. If the office of archdeacon or canon residentiary becomes vacant at the same time as the see, the usual practice is to leave the office unfilled until the new diocesan has been appointed, but the Crown will make an appointment, and cannot be fettered in doing so, if it judges that to be right.

49. Since 1 January 1989, if the office of incumbent of a parish church cathedral has remained unfilled for nine months, the right to appoint the next incumbent who will become provost lapses to the Archbishop of the province. Previously it lapsed to the Crown.

50. When an appointment is made to a deanery, the resultant vacancy does not revert to the Crown, unlike the vacant benefice that is created by the appointment of a diocesan bishop.

Sources of Candidates

51. One of the principal tasks of the AAS, and one that has been constant since the office was established about twenty-five years ago, is the gathering, formally and informally, holding and dissemination of information about priests who are thought to have the capability to fill a major role either in the immediate

future or at some later date. The way in which this is done is constantly evolving and becoming more systematic. Administrative procedures provide for regular review of the information.

52. Advice comes from and is sought from a variety of sources, lay and ecclesiastical. Current practice is that diocesan bishops provide wide-ranging and detailed information on clergy who are thought to have the potential to fill senior posts, indicating for which type of post they might, over time, be appropriately considered. The AAS also collects information informally, for example from members of a bishop's senior staff meeting. In addition, he receives advice about clergy from sources which may include such people as chairmen of diocesan houses of clergy and laity. Those appointed to senior posts may have first come to attention by any of these routes. However, not every appointment is made from among those clergy about whom the AAS has information.

53. When suggestions are made the AAS aims to obtain further opinions as far as possible so as to build up a more rounded picture of the individual. The product of this work can be seen in the proposals offered when a vacancy has to be filled, for all of that source material can be drawn on for the benefit of the appointer. It is the practice of the office not to attribute comments about individuals without prior approval from the provider.

54. The Prime Minister's office keeps its own confidential information separately. This is built up through the extensive consultations undertaken by the PAS and his office in filling not only posts in the hierarchy but also the seven hundred or so benefices in the gift of the Crown or Lord Chancellor.

55. The information kept by the AAS and the confidential information in Downing Street are quite separate and there is no automatic exchange of information between the offices. The Appointments' Secretaries frequently consult one another but only give one another specific material about individual priests if they have first obtained the permission of the original provider. Formally, the systems are in parallel.

56.   Applications from individuals to be considered for the posts referred to in this Appendix are not encouraged and never invited. On the Crown's side, the Crown prerogative to appoint is absolute and not to be compromised. However the PAS very readily makes himself available to meet a priest, whose suitability for appointment to a Crown benefice or to a higher preferment may have been suggested, or who desires to have a general discussion about his future ministry. Similarly, when the Crown is ready to make the offer of a specific appointment, there will be direct contact from the Prime Minister's office to help a priest come to a view about his own wishes in the matter and to ascertain whether the nominee would be ready to take up the office should the invitation be made.

57.   On the Church's side there are occasions when a bishop may discuss with a priest the kinds of role he might occupy at some future date and, as it arises, explore with the priest whether he would wish to be considered for some particular post but practice varies from diocese to diocese. Appraisal or ministerial review discussions provide a context for this to be explored in some instances.

APPENDIX III

Two Papers by Professor Henry Chadwick

Professor Henry Chadwick prepared two papers for us in the course of our work. The first, prepared in March 1989, was in the following terms:

Church Leadership in History and Theology

1. Leadership in the Church is partly determined by specifically Christian norms applicable in particular to the people of God, but is also partly connected with the natural order of creation, i.e. with the way in which human societies generally evolve leadership. In the latter case the grounds on which the community acknowledges a leader's authority may be, first, the personal magnetic power of an individual, an 'Admirable Crichton' so to speak, standing at the periphery of traditional social forms. Personal magnetism need not always be beneficent; with Hitler and with Pastor Jones of Los Angeles and Guyana it was maleficent. Influence over people may be by love and loyalty, but may also be by fear. A successful military leader commands loyalty; he facilitates the tribe's survival. The observation that successful generals seldom make good politicians is as old as Plato (*Euthydemus* 290 D). Commonly societies have been governed by a traditional group of families whose expected role has been to exercise public responsibility and service. However, leaders emerging by charismatic magnetism or by traditional social obligation need the consent and thereby the election of the communities they lead. This is indispensable if they are to have real authority, which does not always articulate the consensus of democratic opinion but must make some unpopular decisions. The power of authority is first manifest when a leader can retain loyalty when imposing a will and a policy upon a community to which they are not congenial or convenient. (E.g. In his vast single-combat against the secularity of the contemporary West, can John Paul II succeed in the endeavour to make *Humanae Vitae* binding? Can Mrs Thatcher succeed in a Britain growingly doubtful about her policies for manufacturing industry, for

education, and for health? Sometimes success is made possible by fear of a worse alternative. Henry VIII could impose his break with Rome on a country hardly at all disposed to be Protestant, because of dread of return to the civil Wars of the Roses; the bribery of redistribution of church lands to courtiers also helped).

2.   For rulers and governors an important source of power and authority has been patronage; the ability to nominate those at the second level, whose positions carry honour, perhaps good remuneration, and probable power and influence. There is no method of selecting which looks just or efficient to persons who wish to be selected and are not chosen. Louis XIV is credited with the sad remark that whenever he made a senior appointment he found himself with a hundred alienated and angry candidates and one person who showed no sign of gratitude. In higher education it is unusual for any appointment to be made which is not then felt to be contentious. The more efficient (i.e. the more meritocratic) the procedure, the greater the grievance in those whose merits have not been recognised.

3.   As Richard Hooker remarked in the famous opening sentence of his *Laws* of *Ecclesiastical Polity*, no ruler or leader can govern without a lot of feeling that it could all be done much better.

4.   In the history of the Church it is easy to see in operation systems of election with close analogies to those in the natural order of society: traditional families or groups of families; charismatic and prophetic leadership that is then given visible legitimacy by a process of election; or a choice by the clergy and people. In the West secular monarchs and bishops of Rome have shown a consistent disinclination to leave the choice of bishops to merely local voters; and since the middle of the nineteenth century the Ultramontane movement in the Roman Catholic Church has much increased centralising pressures. Especially in Germany and Austria local feeling has been disregarded by central authority, and a price is paid for that.

5.   The practice of drawing leaders from a particular family or groups of families can be seen at work in the early Church. It

would not be unnatural to entrust the liturgical leadership of a Christian community to a leading family owning a house with space sufficient for the people to gather in. In the second century, Polycrates Bishop of Ephesus could claim with defensive pride that seven among his close relatives had been bishops. In Mesopotamia and in Armenia in late antiquity and after, it was normal procedure for an episcopal see to remain in the hands of a single family (however extended the concept of the 'family' might be). In the Nile valley it was not at all unusual for church offices, whether bishop, presbyter or deacon, to be in effect (not in canon law) hereditary. In fifth-century Spain, as Pope Hilarus complained in the 460s, bishops were treating their sees as property which they could dispose of in their last will and testament. This was no huge extension of the then widespread practice of getting a dying bishop to nominate his successor, at least as coadjutor with the reversion of the job. It seemed a desirable way of averting faction and even riot when the congregation had to choose a successor. In 499 Pope Symmachus presided over a synod of Italian bishops at Rome that considered, *inter alia*, what the procedure should be when a pope died without having nominated his successor - '*quod absit*'.

6. At the beginning of the fifth century the poet Prudentius from Spain rhapsodised over a family of Valerii who had produced an unbroken line of bishops for Saragossa. Comparable evidence appears for the towns in the Rhône valley. Naturally, those whose families were outside the magic circle were critical. In the third century Origen's 22nd homily on Numbers denounced endemic nepotism in appointments.

7. Origen was an anticlerical high churchman, and his ascetic temper led him to adopt a very detached and at times bitterly scornful estimate of bishops generally, not merely those whose family connection had secured their appointment.[1] The alternative to 'tradition', or hereditary dynasties, was popular election. The legitimacy of the bishop's authority then depended upon the consent of his people, the acclamation and support of the *plebs*.

---

[1] Ambrose of Milan (*Offic.* 1, 44, 218) says 'it is rare for the sons of clergy to be ordained'. In Italy things were clearly different.

8.   The ancient Church soon found that election by the *plebs* was not problem-free. Too frequently it led to factions being formed, and the supporters of one candidate found themselves nursing the most hostile picture of the supporters of a rival candidate. A western council of the year 343 (held at Serdica – Sofia in Bulgaria) recorded its feeling of outrage at the practice of bribing a claque of laity to shout loudly in favour of a particular candidate. Candidates soon found that while it was thought wicked to bribe the electors with private money, it was acceptable to bribe them with the electors' own resources, namely the reserves in the Church chest which could be used to assist the poor with free meals-on-wheels and other benefits. After Constantine's time the local Churches could receive land and property by way of endowment. It became contentious whether or not such endowments could be alienated for the benefit of refugees, and if for refugees, then for the poor generally; and if for the poor generally, then to secure their support in a contested episcopal election. (This was a heated issue in the contested papal election of 498.) The force of group rivalry had its most dramatic manifestation in the papal election of 366, where the supporters of the eventually successful candidate Damasus carried out a violent attack on his rival's supporters, leaving 137 of them dead in the basilica where the consecration was taking place. A pagan city prefect had the task of restoring order and deciding between rivals.

9.   Because the *plebs* were vulnerable to faction, an important role was, from a very early stage, played by the bishops of neighbouring Churches, who came to lay hands upon the candidate at his consecration, and who represented not only their own Churches but the acceptance of the new bishop and his Church in the universal Church world-wide, soon simply called the *catholica*, in distinction from local sects with private deviations from the 'Great Church'. No small part of the aura and respect accruing to the local bishop depended on this catholicity of recognition. To be bishop of a particular sect might be good for one's income if the sect were funded by a well-to-do-banker, but in the long run the sects remained on the shelf, stuck in the past while the Great Church moved with the times. At an episcopal Synod or Council (the early Church made no distinction between

the Greek *synodos* and the Latin *concilium*) the local bishop was the embodiment of his people. To his people he represented the unity and universality of all the Churches bonded in eucharistic communion. The ancient Church developed a system of Church passports, called in Latin *formatae*, which travelling Christians could present as a certificate of their orthodoxy.

10. At a remarkably early stage, in all probability before all the writings now in the New Testament Canon were written, the last of the Twelve had died, and the question of who had the legitimate authority to exercise their pastoral commission was answered by pointing to the succession of bishops presiding over the local Churches, similarly constituting a 'college' like the apostles.

11. The extent to which the independence of the local community was limited was quickly exemplified by the row at Corinth before the end of the first century AD. The Corinthian Christians decided by a substantial majority to sack its clergy and to install a new lot. The implication of the evidence is that women had something to do with the overthrow of the old and the introduction of the new clergy (1 Clement 21, and in ch. 55 the dragging in of biblical women heroes Judith and Esther). There is no suggestion of any doctrinal deviation. The community at Rome commissioned Clement, probably their senior and presiding presbyter, to write to Corinth to remonstrate with the Corinthians for their delusion that the authority and tenure of their pastors rested on the congregation's consent. There was no power of deselection in the case of clergy who had blamelessly offered the gifts and had been installed by clergy appointed by the apostles themselves. The Corinthians had failed to realise that the ordering of the community of the new covenant is no less precise, no less divinely given, than the hierarchical threefold ministry of the Old Testament, with its distinctions of function between priest and laity.

12. For centuries to come the custom, subsequently enshrined in formal Canon Law by Church councils, required election by 'the clergy and people'. Nevertheless, occasional disorders at elections in major sees gave the imperial government a strong

interest in appointments that would not cause riots. Moreover great sees came to acquire endowments, and all property was held under the law of the Emperor and not independent of him. In the Greek East it was unusual for emperors to play any part in episcopal appointments; but in the West of the sixth century, the Merovingian kings insisted on their right to nominate. The godly prince embodied the principle of lay participation. Bishops were influential, and the kings had a political interest in their public role. In the so-called dark ages not so many people were literate. The necessity of reading Bible and liturgical books gave bishops the impetus to provide cathedral schools, once the barbarians destroyed the old. Sometimes the royal nomination was taken to suffice. In twelfth century Ireland Malachi, Bishop of Armagh, found that some of the Irish bishops had been nominated by the High Kings, but had received no ordination to their order and office. They were exercising their office under royal authority alone. A century earlier in Gaul, Fulbert of Chartres refused to attend at the consecrations of three bishops on the ground that, though nominated by royal authority for consecration, the nominations had not received the assent of the clergy and people (*PL* 141. 212-13.)

13.   Already in the legislation of Justinian (*Nov.* 123.1; 137.2) and in the letters of Pope Nicholas I, the laity expected to take part in an episcopal election were the grandees, not the common people.[2] Their role was simply to shout the acclamation. The real choice was made by consultations among small groups of top people. So also among the clergy, the cathedral chapters came (by about 1000) to have a preponderant role in the selection process in the West. They had the advantage of being on the spot when the former bishop died and needed burial: they also formed a coherent body of senior clergy. Rural clergy are not mentioned in accounts of elections in the eleventh century. When the various parties disagreed among themselves (not infrequently), opportunity was increased for royal or papal intervention. In the Carolingian empire the permission of the prince was required for a consecration to proceed (*concessio regalis*, the *congé*). The kings

---

[2] In the Latin churches of ancient North Africa there were 'lay elders' (*seniores laici*) with responsibilities for the church chest and customarily playing a role in the choice of a new bishop.

were frequently tempted to say that if the candidate they preferred were elected, they would gladly grant permission for the consecration. In 921 Pope John X rebuked the Archbishop of Cologne for trying to break the royal prerogative to appoint to the see of Liège.

14.   Medieval monarchs needed to control their bishops because they needed reliable supporters in their struggle to maintain power over against barons. In Germany imperial power over bishops was greater than that exercised by the French kings, who could appoint to comparatively few sees, most being in the hands of dukes. Clerical protests against this lay power of appointment were not very vocal; but the dream of independence was never lost. The men of the Church wanted the clergy and people to have a free choice, and hoped the king would then confirm it. To give the free choice to the clergy and people was to make it more likely that a local priest, say a cathedral canon, would be appointed. A royal appointment tended to take more account of national, or at least of royal, needs, producing political appointments.

15.   For the medieval world the appointment of a person to an office was normally symbolised by a physical act signifying the giving of authority. The symbol of a bishop's pastoral authority was his staff. At his consecration, the metropolitan and consecrating bishops laid hands on his head saying 'Receive the Holy Spirit' (*Accipe Spiritum Sanctum*). But the new bishop in the ninth century also received the staff (*accipe baculum*). Gradually kings began to send a newly appointed bishop the staff as a symbol of his jurisdiction, the exercise of which would receive royal support. In Germany the episcopal ring[3] was also conferred by the Emperor. The meaning was not in doubt: the temporal prince was investing the bishop with authority, and the distinction between temporal and spiritual was wholly blurred. Eleventh-century reformers made an issue of lay 'investiture'. The zeal of the reformers was enhanced by anger at the practice of princes of

---

[3] The ring is attested as a mark of episcopal authority by Isidore of Seville in the seventh century (*Offic. eccl.* 2, 5, 12). In antiquity and in medieval times a signet ring was no luxury, but a necessity for the authentication of letters by persons of authority.

claiming the revenues of vacant sees for their privy purse and then keeping sees vacant.

16.   Secular princes naturally demanded of the new bishop an oath of homage. The bishop was a vassal and must know it. This medieval practice still prevails in England. It presupposes some distrust.[4]

17.   It was an old Germanic axiom that the owner of the land also exercised religious control. In the later Roman empire the bishops encouraged great landowners to build churches on their estates and to provide for the priest and the cost of the light and heat. The proprietary church (*Eigenkirche*) could then have an uneasy relation to the diocese and its bishop. Moreover, we hear of great landowners who persuaded the bishop to ordain one of their minor servants to be priest to the estate, so that some priests might also be expected to serve as ostlers to their lord. Agobard of Lyons judged this development an insult to the dignity of the sacred ministry.

18.   The struggle of the medieval Church in the West for greater freedom from lay domination (receiving classic expression for the English in Magna Carta *ut ecclesia anglicana libera sit*) became fused with the tension between the national Church and the universal Church, of which the *cathedra Petri* was the symbol. The see of Rome reinforced the authority of local bishops by embodying a universality greater than the merely regional and ethnic concerns of the secular prince. Hence the rising tension (a major ingredient, besides the problem of land ownership, in the background to the English Reformation) between canon lawyers and common lawyers, with the incisive claim by the latter that where Canon and Statute Law are in conflict, Canon Law is without authority. (This thesis is argued by Christopher St German, 1460-1541).

19.   Henry VIII's Act of 1538 on the appointment of bishops (still in legal force even if in practice the Prime Minister now

---

[4] Diocesan bishops promise loyalty to the metropolitan. Matthew Parker in 1559 was the first Archbishop of Canterbury not to swear loyalty to the Pope. Cranmer did so, though with qualifications.

allows the Church to define the field of choice) eliminates the Pope from the appointing of bishops, and reduces the election by cathedral chapter to something purely nominal. The latter reduction was not out of line with what had often occurred in medieval Catholic Europe. In practice, the kings of France since 1300 had scarcely tolerated any papal say in episcopal appointments there. Henry might have escaped excommunication if he had not killed John Fisher and entitled himself head of the Church. Henry thereby transferred papal authority to himself; he did not abolish it. In 1540 the too obsequious Cranmer could suggest that all episcopal authority was derived exclusively from the Crown, not from the apostolic commission by ordination; indeed, he thought, the apostles had acted *faute de mieux* in appointing clergy only because they had no Christian princes to whom to turn. Richard Hooker had a different view: consecration by duly ordained bishops in the authentic succession was needed, and the action of the Crown made it possible for the implied jurisdiction to be exercised but was not its source of authority. Hooker also argued that the authority of Queen Elizabeth over the Church was in no sense identical with that once exercised by the successor of St Peter at Rome. But he defended the Crown's right to nominate bishops; he observed that Philip II of Spain had agreed to publish the decrees of the Council of Trent in his Netherlands dominions with the proviso that there was no prejudice or diminution to his customary rights of appointment to ecclesiastical offices. Under the Concordat, the President of France has power to nominate Roman Catholic bishops in Alsace and Lorraine. This is still the position. Hooker's remark about Philip of Spain illustrates the point that senior church appointments by the Crown are not in principle different from less senior appointments.

20. Biblical patterns of ministry are not monolithic. In the Old Testament ministerial authority serves the Law (Torah) mediated through Moses. Aaron and the Levitical priesthood maintain the daily service of the Tabernacle, then of the Temple; the Psalter is as noble a monument of that way of worship as can be found. Beside the priesthood (in Ezekiel's case overlapping with it) stands the prophetic movement, at times critical of the compromises that the priests have accepted with the wishes of the people,

but in principle reinforcing loyalty to the Temple worship, the keeping of both ceremonial and moral law, and not as such challenging the ministerial role of the sons of Levi.

21. Among the first generations of Christians the primary pattern of ministry is given by the Lord himself, who came not to be ministered unto but to minister and give his life . . . But the pastoral care of the flock, the proclamation of the gospel, the safeguarding of authentic teaching and ethical discipline, are inherent in the apostolic commission. From the Corinthian epistles it is certain that there was some very early debate about the identity of those who did or did not have this commission. The claims of Paul were not self-evident for everyone. The apostles had an unrepeatable and intransmissible function, namely of bearing direct witness to the Lord and his Resurrection. But other functions of pastoral responsibility were transmitted to serve ensuing generations. A permanence of function passes into the nature of an order within the structure of the Church. The possession of acknowledged and legitimate pastors is crucial for both unity and continuity in the ongoing life of the community. Moreover, the pastoral functions require sustained training. But to speak of the episcopate, or presbyterate, or the diaconate, as an order does not mean that such a distinctive ministry has an existence apart from the community which it is called to serve.

22. For Ignatius of Antioch the bishop is the focus of the eucharistic fellowship, and it is a disruption of Christian unity to hold separate eucharists apart from the bishop and his presbyters (*Magn.* 7. 1-2). This personal focus is, for Ignatius, that which is a condition of authenticity in the sacraments; his epistles first speak of the eucharist in communion with the bishop and his presbyters as being 'valid' (the sense of this term is not yet juridical). For the ancient Church of the patristic age the celebration of the eucharist was (as it is for Anglican eucharistic liturgy also) a sharing of the worship of the heavenly host, a representation on earth of the self-offering of the Lord to the Father. So also the celebrating bishop, 'presiding in love', is never a solitary figure. He teaches from his cathedra, flanked by his presbyters. When, in consequence of St Paul's veto on Christian litigation in secular courts before pagan magistrates (who in the Church 'count for

nothing'), early Christian bishops arbitrated in disputes, they never sat on their own, but were always assisted by their presbyters and deacons (*Didascalia* 2, 47: *Apost. Const.* 2, 47). At the same time the second century bishop is seen both by his own people and by other local Churches as the representative figure in whom the local community have their voice to speak to the wider fellowship. His ordination by the visiting bishops from other local Churches of the province is a sign and instrument of the continuing life and togetherness of the communities.

23. The second-century argument of the orthodox against gnostics, who claimed private lines for the interpretation of scripture, insisted on the mind of the community, visibly controllable by the teaching of publicly identifiable bishops in a known succession, the names of which can be given. The succession is secondary to that of the community, which it serves. And any bishop who deviates from the apostolic tradition embodied in scripture and the tradition of catechesis in the rule of faith and the baptismal creed puts himself outside the authentic succession. The tactile succession *by itself* is not a guarantee.

24. Early in the fourth century, Eusebius of Caesarea writes of the three great offices of Christ, as prophet, priest and king. The bishop, whose task is to proclaim the Gospel, has not only to represent his people to other Churches and to God in intercession, but also to bring God's forgiveness and renewal to his people by word and sacrament. Ordination is in essence distinct from, say, investing a magistrate with the insignia of office. It is a calling by God through his Church, the body of Christ, in which, in response to the Church's prayer and under the visible sign of the imposition of hands, the person ordained receives a spiritual charism for the task. In the name of Christ, or (as St Paul put it in 2 Cor. 2. 19) 'in the person of Christ', the ordained minister represents by his pastorate the Chief Shepherd who is Christ himself (1 Peter 5.2-4). Any title applied to the pastor, including 'pastor' itself, is so used because he is the minister of Christ commissioned to act and speak in the Lord's name. So he is to exercise *episkope*, to exercise the judgement of a senior person or presbyter, to serve in *diakonia*, and in all these functions to be an earthly embodiment of the Lord in Heaven. The Greek churches

by the end of the second century are found calling the bishop *hiereus,* the Latin churches use *sacerdos.* These terms at that date carried a less 'sacerdotal' meaning than modern, post-Reformation writers assume. Augustine of Hippo is the earliest writer to express reserves about 'priestly' titles, partly because of possible Levitical associations, partly because all Christians constitute a priestly body (*City of God* 20. 10). When separated Donatists declared that 'purity is indispensable in a priest so that he can obtain from God blessings which his lay people are not worthy to win', Augustine objected (on Ps. 36. 2. 20). Augustine liked to tell his people that he taught them not as their master but as a fellow pupil of their divine Master (S. 292. 1). 'To you I am a shepherd, but to the Chief Shepherd I am a sheep together with you' (on Ps. 126.3). His priestly function is to be intercessor, and the 'dispenser of God's word and sacraments'. 'The bishop put over the people must know that he is their servant.' (S Guelf 32. 1 'a bad bishop is not really a bishop, any more than a beggar called Felix is happy').

25. Accountability in the case of lapses by senior clergy has at no time in church history been the easiest problem to solve. In the ancient Church a bishop from whom his brother bishops withdrew their communion and recognition was in effect deposed, though it often required action by civil authority to expel the delinquent or heretic. Alcoholism was far from an unknown concomitant of episcopal hospitality. Imprudent hugs to women in spiritual distress could lead on to embarrassments. Fiddling the accounts of the church chest could also occur. 1 Timothy 5. 8 said that a bishop had a duty to provide for his household, and medieval popes and bishops took the exhortation seriously. When Innocent IV conferred a Lincoln canonry on his nephew, Bishop Grosseteste declared both his reverence for papal authority and his clear conviction that so corrupt an act could come only from Antichrist, so that he was unable to accept it.

26. Good administration is about people, and is pastoral in character; it is not or ought not to be in the Church merely the possession of a good filing system. Admittedly, administrative incompetence can make things awkward. If a diocesan director of education and schools is bad at the job, a bishop who brings a

competent person to work *side by side* with the incompetent probably causes much chaos: no one knows who to put a question to. (Authority amazingly invited Bishop Agnellus Andrew to take charge of Vatican TV and Radio without requiring his aged predecessor to resign; the consequences for Bishop Agnellus and everyone concerned were awful.)

27. Dioceses have different criteria for their needs in a new bishop, and we now have Vacancy-in-See committees to try to formulate the relevant criteria. There is often a choice to be made between a candidate who will be something of a national figure, active in the Lords, chairing CRAC for the broadcasters, chairing committees on test-tube infants or abortion or other moral issues, and a candidate who will be a close pastor to his priests and people. They are often not incompatible criteria. Is it for the working party on senior appointments to prescribe here? Probably not. If a diocese has good archdeacons, it is no doubt more important that the bishop be a holy man, a good pastor, and a thoughtful speaker and writer than that he be a competent committee man. The relationship between a bishop and his diocesan synod will probably vary in individual cases, and cannot easily be put into a straitjacket.

28. That a clergyman should be ordained for a specific pastoral task in a named place rather than *in vacuo* is laid down by a canon of the ecumenical council of Chalcedon (451), much cited in medieval canonists in the West perhaps aware of a growing tendency to push its provisions aside. A bishop is to exercise *episkope* in relation to a community, and the title is not an honorific decoration but a huge responsibility. (Honorific titles are justified so far as they remind the holders of that responsibility.) So when bishops came to find their dioceses so large that they needed suffragans to help them, the suffragans were given a named town as their see. (Modern Anglican practice makes the town one already within the diocese, but in earlier Pre-Reformation times the see of a suffragan bishop of Winchester might be e.g. Sidon or some place now *in partibus infidelium*.) Suffragan bishops, like the 'country bishops' or *chorepiscopi* of the Greek Orthodox tradition have frequently been somewhat unhappy. The record in church history is one in which there is

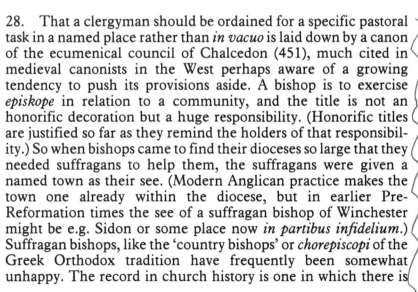

some degree of discomfort and malaise, probably because a suffragan bishop instinctively draws to himself a family of souls to whom he wishes to be Father in God, and simultaneously knows that jurisdiction (or the responsibility to sort things out when a scandal occurs) lies with someone else. Nevertheless diocesan bishops would be swamped by overwork if they did not have such assistance.

29.   If a diocesan bishop ceased to have a decisive voice in the choice of his suffragans and archdeacons, a difficult job might be made a great deal harder. Sometimes, however, the suffragans and archdeacons chosen by a bishop's predecessor turn out to be more supportive than his own choices. Admittedly it is far from unknown for a new bishop to find his policy (e.g. in merging livings) publicly attacked in letters to the press by one of his archdeacons inherited from his predecessor. (An archdeacon of his own choice might have done such a thing too perhaps?) A person mature enough to be made a diocesan bishop may be presumed to have learnt to co-operate with colleagues with whom there may be disagreements during the staff meeting.

30.   The early Church's emphasis on the role of the local people in the choice of their new bishop suggests that they saw wisdom in consultations with lay people. As I have said above, there was already in ancient times a tendency for the laity consulted to be persons of influence and substance. Senior lay people in a Diocesan Synod are commonly people with experience of making things work. It seems common prudence that some of them at least should be invited to send in their views if they so wish. One cannot say that there is a theological principle in this, other than the general ecclesiological principle that the Church does not consist of the clergy alone.

31.   It is, however, a relevant fact that a diocesan bishop (and a suffragan bishop also) commonly have more than an evangelistic and sacramental and pastoral role. They have a social role – hospitality; reconciliation of polarised quarrelling groups like management and labour; looking after educational institutions and hospitals in the diocese; providing a voice for the poor and marginalised. The primitive Christian mission in the Gentile

world, as early as St Paul's time, was centred on towns (the countryside long remained 'secular', and the conversion of the peasants was very slow), and so to this day the diocesan organisation of the Church places the cathedral and the bishop in an urban setting. A bishop is understood by many in his city to have some public representational role for that city, and may well have a higher public profile than the Lord Mayor. If he has an institution of higher education in his diocese, he will inevitably have some part in the life of that, and it is important that, without any need for the bishop himself to be 'academic', he should nevertheless be capable of utterance on major issues which Christian teachers in the university are not embarrassed to hear him say. In the *Confessions*, Book 13, Augustine insists that the discernment of Christian truth is a gift to all believers, not merely to the clergy.

32. No method of choosing senior clergy in the Church has yet been found which leaves everyone content. The Provost of Sheffield invites the Working Party (see Appendix IV) to think it possible that past procedures have been wrong, and that is fine as long as the working party does not think that any changes or new procedures it may recommend and succeed in getting implemented are sure or even likely to be regarded as improvements, not to say solving the problem. We shall always have some people who feel it could be better done.

Professor Chadwick prepared a second paper for us in April 1992 as follows:

Some Theological and Historical Considerations

1. The first holders of authority in the Church were Christ's apostles, 'sent' and commissioned by the Lord himself. The apostles were not only the primary witnesses to the Resurrection and to the commission they had received but also the source of pastoral authority and government in the Churches which their mission founded. From the letters of Paul it is easy to see that there was controversy about his own standing as an apostle –

controversy which he saw as inherent in the simultaneous debate about the mission of the Church into the Gentile world. In that momentous enterprise he needed the support and recognition of the 'pillar' apostles at Jerusalem, or he would have 'run in vain' (Gal. 2.2) – a text which presupposes that the apostolic mission was a collective programme and not a loose series of disconnected individualistic activities. So Paul recognised the special authority of the Twelve (1 Cor. 15.5) who had accompanied the Lord during his earthly ministry and were chosen by him – a fact recorded in all four canonical gospels (Matthew 10, Mark 3, Luke 6 and John 1) and again in Acts 1.13. Matthew 19.28 shows that their number consciously corresponded to that of the tribes of Israel. The importance of the Twelve can be seen in the narrative of Acts 1, where their number is made up after the defection of Judas Iscariot. Two candidates were proposed, Justus and Matthias: one was chosen, and one may wonder about the feelings of the one who was not. In the Revelation (21.14) the walls of the heavenly Jerusalem have twelve foundation stones, each with the name of one of the Twelve.

2.   In St Paul's catalogue of God's gifts to the Church (1 Cor. 12.28) the apostles stand at the head of the list. The title-deeds of the Church consist in the commission given to those sent by the Lord, a charism conferring the power to carry out the task assigned. A similar list appears in Ephesians 4.11. Both in 1 Corinthians and in Ephesians the primary role of the apostle is to act as a bond of authority and unity in the Christian body. Together with Christian prophets, the apostles constitute the foundation of the building, in which Christ is the chief corner-stone (Eph. 2.20).

3.   The theme of an apostolic foundation reappears in the commission to St Peter of Matthew 16.18: 'You are Peter and on this rock I will build my Church.' This foundation-authority is underlined by the conferring of the power of the keys: entrance to the Kingdom is by gates which are controlled. The ancient rabbis spoke of binding and loosing in reference to synagogue discipline. In Matthew's Gospel the power is entrusted to Peter; in John's Gospel (20.22-23) it is entrusted to all the apostles. In Matthew 18.18 the commission is given to the community as a whole.

Their decisions on earth will be ratified in heaven. So the Church is a community with ministerial organs of decision guarding against error.

4.   The historical witness of the apostles to what Jesus said and did is theirs alone and, in the ordinary sense, they had and could have no successors in that respect. This element of uniqueness, of intransmissibility, in the apostles is inherent in their witness to the Lord and his teaching, and it is acknowledged by all subsequent Christian conviction in the axiom that the essential message of the Church in every generation is identical with the apostolic gospel. The process of forming the canon of the New Testament writings shows this presupposition at work in the life of the Church in the second half of the second Christian century. It can also be seen in the fact that we possess virtually no significant records about the words and actions of Jesus which are not cast in the form of a confession of faith in him as the messianic inaugurator of the Kingdom of God. Only familiarity obscures for us how startling is the phenomenon that the earliest Christians expressed their faith in Christ by telling the story of his biography. That story was the apostolic witness, and a high proportion of it concerned the passion and resurrection of the Lord.

5.   The Lord's commission to Peter and to the other apostles presupposes that the Church will not die out. The continuing life of the Church entailed the need for a continuing authority; that is, for ministers inheriting the apostolic commission to proclaim the gospel and simultaneously to safeguard the unity of the community. In the first Church in Jerusalem, the mother of all churches, this authority was especially located in James the Lord's brother, side by side with the apostolic 'college' in which Peter had a leading position. The model provided by James' position may have contributed towards the emergence of a single pastor with oversight (*episkope*) in the local community. During the first and early second centuries, there were regional diversities. In some places leadership was held by a group of elders or 'presbyters' (Acts 20.17).

6.   At Philippi there were 'bishops and deacons' (Phil. 1.1),

evidently in a position of leadership in the local community. The reference is something of a surprise when one recalls how the letters of St Paul, outside the Pastoral Epistles to Timothy and Titus, have little to say about permanent ministerial offices: the emphasis lies on the Spirit, creator of both order and vitality. The highly charismatic group at Corinth was short on order but strong on vitality. Texts in 2 Corinthians suggest that they (or at least some of them) resented Paul's apostolic authority. He needed to assure them that in his understanding his authority was entrusted by God to set free, not to dominate and enslave (1.24; 10.8). But without order there can be no real freedom.

7. The death of the apostles left the Churches at risk in an uncertain world. The challenges to the ministerial leadership which found itself coping with the vacuum made it natural to form written texts composed in the name of apostles, especially (for the Gentile Churches) St Paul. In the epistles to Timothy and Titus directions in the name of an authority uncompromised by the contemporary disputes told the Churches how to choose their ministers, the criteria and moral qualities needed, and, by clear implication, what should be done to commission them. Usually the congregation was very active in expressing its mind about the choice of minister to be its pastor, but the commission was conveyed by laying on of hands, accompanied by prayer (for the gift and power of the Holy Spirit); and this symbolic action was a visible instrument by which the recipient received the divine 'gift' transmitted from apostolic authority (Acts 13.3; 6.6; especially 1 Tim. 4.14 and 2 Tim. 1.6).

8. In the letters to Timothy and Titus the presbyters are plural, the bishop singular. Even if the latter usage is generic, the usage suggests that if, at this stage of development, all bishops might also be numbered among the body of presbyters, not all presbyters had the oversight associated with the function and office of a bishop. The qualities required for episcopal oversight include not only deep study of the scriptures (i.e. the Old Testament) but also natural capacities of leadership and common sense (1 Tim. 3.3-7 and Titus 1.6-9). Of some special interest is the stress on the requirement (1 Tim. 3.7) that a candidate for the position of bishop 'be held in good repute by outsiders'. Even at this relatively

early stage of the Church's development, the bishop had a high public 'profile' or visibility in his town. The respect in which the Christian community was held in society at large was bound up with the esteem in which non-Christians held their acknowledged leader. Already in embryo we meet here the tension between the domestic internal responsibility of the bishop and the public social role, which was to become mountingly important as a factor in the selection of candidates for episcopal office.

9.   Presbyters or elders were expected to exercise leadership and rule in the congregation. But from 1 Timothy 5.17 it appears that not all were expected to teach, and preach, since among the presbyters there are some who are to receive a double proportion of the offerings of the faithful on the ground of their labours in preaching and teaching. While the letters of Ignatius of Antioch speak in high terms of the bishop in relation to God and in relation to his people, Ignatius uses language hardly less exalted for the role of presbyters who are the bishop's council. They sit on either side of the bishop in the apse and in his absence they may baptise, consecrate and bless or even preach. If the bishop was present when they performed these sacred functions, that was by delegation. Whereas deacons (who, like the laity, stood and did not sit during the liturgy) were ordained by the bishop acting alone, presbyters shared in the laying on of hands at the ordination of a presbyter. The early participation of the city presbyters in the laying on of hands of a new bishop at Alexandria was changed to bring that Church into line with the other sister Churches of the Roman world. Early Christian Churches were urban, and extension into the countryside was slow. Where a rural or village congregation was established, that was usually after the landowner had become a Christian, and then pastoral responsibility was often entrusted to a presbyter or, in some areas, to a 'country bishop' whose powers were subordinate to the diocesan bishop based in the nearby town. As counsellors to the bishop, presbyters had a recognised part to play of considerable importance. In the third century Cyprian of Carthage was reluctant to make any important decisions except on the basis of consensus among his presbyters, and he found this hard to carry out when five of the presbyters formed a hard core of implacable opposition (*Ep.* 14.4). His contemporary Cornelius, bishop of

Rome, had a similar policy and found similar difficulty with local opposition (*Ep.* 49). It was also normal procedure for presbyters to share with their bishop in disciplinary decisions, e.g. when a clergyman's doctrine or behaviour incurred censure or suspension. In several ancient Councils presbyters sat and voted together with their bishops.

10.   Deacons were personal assistants to bishops, with special responsibilities not only for the Gospel or the Cup at the eucharist but also for caring of the poor by the distribution of alms in kind or in cash. The senior or principal deacon, by the fourth century entitled the 'archdeacon', was not originally a presbyter. In fourth-century Rome there were only seven deacons, in closer touch with the bishop (and better paid) than the presbyters, and a presbyter was ordained only on the recommendation of a deacon (Jerome, *Ep.* 146.2); from this developed the custom whereby the archdeacon presents candidates for ordination.

11.   The custom by which the archdeacon of Canterbury acts for the Archbishop in installing new bishops in the province is as old as St Anselm's time (Eadmer, *Historia Novorum IV*, p. 196, ed. Rule).

Cathedral Chapters

12.   In time the cathedral church in the town where the bishop had the chair symbolising his teaching office and responsibility became too much for the bishop, and its daily worship and fabric became the duty of presbyters or monks assigned to this church. In mediaeval England, monks provided for Canterbury, Carlisle, Durham, Ely, Norwich, Rochester, Winchester and Worcester. Other cathedrals (Chichester, Exeter, Hereford, Lichfield, Lincoln, London, Salisbury, Wells, York) were staffed by secular clergy. After Henry VIII's dissolution of the religious orders, all cathedrals were the responsibility of secular presbyters.

13.   By the eighth century the body of cathedral clergy began to acquire a corporate independence, and became known as the chapter, *capitulum*, in time presided over by a dean. Normally

there was a precentor in charge of the music; a chancellor, expected to be a theologian interested in education; a treasurer to care for endowments and fabric. Some of the canons resided by the cathedral, others did not. It became usual for the archdeacon to be associated in the responsibility for the Cathedral. The Dean and Chapter gradually became distinct from the other urban clergy and in some degree independent even of the bishop, who would come to the cathedral for high festivals and ordinations, but remained the authority with jurisdiction in the event of a disciplinary problem. When the bishop died, the cathedral clergy were on the spot to see to his funeral and also to elect a successor – a custom becoming established in the West in the eleventh century. Although by the thirteenth century the power of nomination was recognised as belonging to cathedral chapters, in practice the nomination of a new bishop usually rested with the sovereign, and it was unusual for a cathedral chapter or the archbishop or the pope not to concur with the royal nomination.

14.   Henry VIII left the power of electing a new bishop in the hands of cathedral chapters, subject to the severe penalties of Praemunire if they failed to elect the person the sovereign nominated.

15.   A generation later the cathedral clergy became the target of vehement criticism from the Puritans, and during the seventeenth century troubles the normal life of cathedrals was severely disrupted. Great changes first came to the English cathedrals with the Ecclesiastical Commission and the Act of Parliament of 1840 which suppressed non-resident prebends, and with exceptions allowed four canonries to each cathedral. The provision that all deans are appointed by the Sovereign dates from this Act of 1840.

16.   The controversies of the sub-apostolic age, the conflict with gnosticism in the second century, and the debate about Montanist prophecy combined to produce a natural emphasis on the continuing ministry as a visible, public guardian of the authentic apostolic tradition. The local bishop represented his people in correspondence with other Churches, and had responsibility for hospitality to visiting representatives from elsewhere. The bishop

therefore embodied for his people a symbol of their membership in a universal body extended in space, as well as in an apostolic society continuing in time. When a local Church needed a new bishop, the bishops from neighbouring Churches in the province would go to lay hands on the person selected by the local people.

17.   The bishops of the first three centuries were local people, chosen by the people from their own number and normally from those who were either deacons or priests. The choice of a layman was possible, but likely only if that layman was obviously the kind of person to meet the pastoral requirement of being 'held in good repute by outsiders' – Cyprian of Carthage being a case in point. Some of the bishops had little formal education (a third-century bishop of Rome was an emancipated slave), but they had the advantage of being respected and of not being outsiders to their people, who were directly involved in the selection. But local congregations did not always make ideal choices. The anxieties contained in Timothy 3.1-7 imply that persons not always discreet, temperate and peaceable had been put forward in some places. So the visiting bishops from other Churches came to exercise a degree of control, and this control was especially weighted in the presiding consecrator, who was usually either the bishop with the greatest length of service as a bishop or the incumbent of the principal city or metropolis of the civil province. The Council of Nicaea invested a power of veto in the metropolitan and also required a minimum of three consecrating bishops if the entire body of the province found it impossible to be present. Accordingly, the power and involvement of the local congregation was gradually diminished in favour of the provincial bishops, especially the metropolitan. Nevertheless the local community long retained a balancing power of veto. As early as the year 314 a Council at Ankara had to legislate for situations where the consecrating bishops laid hands on a person chosen by themselves, who was not acceptable to the community for whom he was intended as pastor.

18.   The direct involvement of the local congregation in the choice of their new bishop was an ideal often marred by rivalries and factions, especially in large cities where the position of bishop soon became one sought for reasons not exclusively religious.

There were social factors too. Rivalries in great cities like Rome, Antioch, or Alexandria could produce disorder in the streets, requiring intervention by civil authority to restore peace. The fourth-century growth of an alliance between Church and Emperor encouraged a more evident interest by the secular power in the choice of bishops in large cities. The individual bishop was slowly coming to be seen not merely as the representative pastor of a local congregation but no less as the representative of a universal, empire-wide organisation to which magistrates looked for help in the suppression of dissidence and disorder. In the eyes of the government of the empire, the Church was valuable social cement (as long as it remained united in itself), and especially useful in inculcating honesty in trade and fidelity in marriage – areas where the lawcourts were notoriously inefficient. Nomination of bishops by the Emperor was very rare. (The earliest known *congé d'élire*, written in gold ink, is of about AD 435). But both local congregations and metropolitans thought it valuable to have bishops who could effectively intercede for their people with the secular governors. In the sixth century in Merovingian Gaul, it became common for bishops to be directly nominated by the Frankish kings.

19. In the Greek East, the great patriarchs (Alexandria, Antioch, Constantinople, Jerusalem) came to have considerable influence upon the choice of bishops. In the West a similar function was performed by the western patriarch at Rome, and the Roman see endeavoured to support local bishops in the barbarian kingdoms and to prevent them becoming mere puppets of a secular government. In medieval western kingdoms there was high tension between secular and ecclesiastical authority, which crystallised in the controversy about rights of investiture. Whether the nominating authority was king or pope, there was a tendency for the local interest in the diocese to yield to centralising power. Election by clergy and people became an election by the cathedral chapter, whose choice, long before Henry VIII's time, was determined for them by the Sovereign acting as representative of the lay interest.

20. The struggle of the medieval Church in the West for freedom from princely domination became entwined with the

conflict between the national and the universal Church (the latter symbolised by papal power). In England, the Act of 1534 on the appointment of bishops removed the papal role, and reduced the election by the cathedral chapter to a purely nominal part of the process. Nevertheless although in 1540 Cranmer suggested that all episcopal authority was derived exclusively from the Sovereign, not from the apostolic commission by ordination, this view was never generally accepted. The Church's view (most clearly articulated by Richard Hooker) was, and remains, that consecration by duly ordained bishops in the authentic tradition was essential. The action of the Sovereign made it possible for the bishop's implied jurisdiction to be exercised, but was not its source of authority.

APPENDIX IV

A Paper by the Provost of Sheffield

The following paper by the Very Revd John Gladwin was prepared for us in March 1989.

Making Appointments in the Church

1. One of the important principles of Anglicanism asserts that the Church has the right and duty to order its own life provided that such ordering does not contravene the values and dynamic of the Gospel. We are not bound to imitate either the patterns found in the Scriptures or to continue what has been the custom in the past. So we can neither hide behind the text of the New Testament nor seek the protection of tradition from a rigorous examination of the question of the proper ordering of ministry in our own time (see Articles 20 and 34).

2. The Bible and tradition act as tests of our work. We have no authority to undermine the teaching of Scripture or to act in a way which severs our link with the Christian community down the ages. Whatever we propose, therefore, needs to keep faith with the Gospel as the Scriptures teach it and with the life of the Church as God has used it throughout history. In matters concerning ministry there are boundaries to our liberty.

3. The Articles also make it clear that the Church is capable of getting these matters wrong. It is possible that we might judge some of the systems for selection and maintenance of ministry in the past as being at odds with the Gospel. There have been periods in history where social position has played too large a part in the ministry of the Church and where systems of remuneration have been too dependent on unregenerate secular models rather than on the values of the Gospel. It is particularly important for an established Church, with a history of such close links with the given order of society, to reflect on what it is doing in the light of the Gospel.

4.   It is also important for a Church with such long traditions as ours to consider what is happening in the rest of the community. We may be drifting on in patterns of life which take their meaning from customs and wisdom of an age which has gone. So we have a double-edged task: to dig into the resources of faith and test our customs and also to look at what is happening elsewhere. The Gospel and the world are to be our agenda. Put theologically, we are working with the resources of creation and of redemption. The Church, as an institution in history, bridges both. It is in the world but called not to be of the world. The ordering of ministry in the Church is one area where we are to seek to hold these two polarities of our life together.

5.   The Church has often laid stress on the given nature of the created order. This can sometimes be at the expense of the innovative and dynamic side of creation. The world is a living world and the story of human life within the world is one of change and diversity. The journey goes on. In it we discover new things and new skills. This is all part of life in a world made and sustained by the life and power of God. One of the most important areas of discovery in our own age has taken place in the field of the human sciences. We have come to new understandings about human behaviour and relationships. These insights have influenced many aspects of the way we approach choices in human life. From the dynamics of human development, through insights into family relationships, and on into ways of managing and supporting people in their various tasks, we have deployed the new insights gained from these spheres of knowledge.

6.   Many tools have been refined in helping to develop our understanding of personality and skills. These have been proven in their use in our community as helping a better understanding of ourselves and of those with whom we may be living or working. These insights have gradually made their way into the life of the Church. They are possibly at their strongest in the work done in selecting people for ministry. They are beginning to affect support of the clergy in the growing use of systems of appraisal. Yet we might well question how seriously the Church takes these insights, which may properly be related to its convictions about

creation, in view of the lack of professional commitment which is sometimes shown in our own practice.

7. The tools of understanding about human behaviour are not restricted to matters concerning individual personality and development. They cover social behaviour as well. Thus we know how the forces of racial and sexual discrimination affect people – including how they are or are not selected for senior posts – and we are learning some ways of overcoming this by a more professional approach. Much of the materials and procedures surrounding equal opportunities are in this area. Proper systems of training, monitoring and supporting people are designed to improve the organisation's performance with regard to people who might otherwise be excluded. It would be salutary for the Church to study what other large agencies do concerning the selection of people for posts. Their rigour both in the area of personal aptitudes and of social forces often make our efforts look somewhat amateur.

8. When we apply these matters to the specific area of management, the selection of people for posts is seen to be a skill in management which nature does not necessarily bestow on all managers. It is a skill for which people can improve their performance by training, assessment of their performance and a general monitoring of the way the organisation is carrying out its responsibilities. Crucial to success is the choice of the right people to hold the senior positions. Thus training and the development of skills has to begin at the top. The tone is thereby set for the whole organisation and carries its way through every level.

9. Thinking and practice concerning the selection of people might be considered under a number of heads.

i. The dissemination of information

What is to be said about the post?
What message is to be conveyed in what is said?
Who do we want to hear the message?

What sort of people are we looking for?
etc. etc.

ii. Discerning the information fed back

Who is to assess what is offered by people who respond?
How is such information to be used and for what?
How do we arrive at such a short list?

iii. Making decisions

Who makes the choices?
What may be asked and what may not?
Guarding against the intrusion of irrelevant or unfair considerations.
The way to approach the person you wish to see appointed.

These questions are just the tip of the iceberg. Questions serve a useful purpose in pressing us to be rigorous and professional in our approach.

10. Such systems are rooted in a commitment to *fairness* which is to ensure that all who might have an interest in a post have equal access to it. They serve to guard against the deployment of prejudices – either consciously or unconsciously. They seek to effect this by identifying the type of unwarranted personal interests and intrusions which might unduly influence the way decisions are made. I have seen, for example, predominantly male interview panels consider excluding married female candidates on the grounds that their family and domestic responsibilities might prevent them giving satisfactory attention to the post.

11. The contemporary professional concern to ensure good practice in making appointments has a double edge. It is concerned for the structures by which appointments are made and with the personal qualities of those who make the appointments. Structural issues concern the management of power in institutions. They seek to ensure that those who make decisions represent a reasonable balance of interest and that the way posts are set up is non-prejudicial. In the Church rigorous questions will need to be asked about who and by what means

decisions are made. Since we are talking about the exercise of power we are bound to ask about accountability. To whom are those who exercise their power accountable? Once we start to ask about accountability we need to ask about things like openness and confidentiality (as opposed to privacy and secrecy).

12. We may begin to apply these concerns to particular sets of appointments in the Church. A bishop, for example, is not just to be seen in the context of a particular diocese but as one who holds an order of ministry in and for the whole Church. The interests of the whole Church in these matters have been held on to by the most tenuous of links. The last vestiges may be seen in the formal acclamation at a bishop's consecration. Yet the question remains, how is the interest of the whole Church to be present and seen to be preserved? Is it true that suffragan bishops are really the personal choice of the diocesan? Is this like the appointment of a curate? In appointments of this nature there are a range of interests to be brought together. These include the interests of the diocesan bishop, the diocese itself and the wider Church. All of this will not function effectively if the processes by which people are considered do not permit wide access and open discussion.

13. This latter comment leads into another fruitful area of theological reflection. When we are talking about appointments to senior posts in the Church of God we are discussing how we fallible humans are able to discern the mind of God for the Church. We are debating the work of the Holy Spirit who alone calls and equips people for ministry. When we consider the vocational work of the Holy Spirit as set out in the Scriptures we might well be impressed by the insight that God's thoughts and ways are not our ways. In the Scriptures that insight is not an encouragement to us to abandon professional rigour in our search. Quite the reverse. It reminds us of our blinkered vision. Our view is much more restricted than God's. It is all too easy for us to allow our own prejudices to shut the door on the person God has chosen. Many are the incidents in the Bible, including Jesus himself, when the person chosen by God is about the last person who will have emerged from the processes of human choice at the time. 'Can any good thing come out of Nazareth?' Time and again God chooses the unexpected person – the Davids of this

world who were left caring for the sheep whilst the powers that be went through the predictable lists! Thus it is vital that the fallible processes of human choice are as wide and as open as possible. Moreover, it should not be possible to predict the outcome. Any candidates should be able to emerge. God should have the room to surprise us by drawing our attention to talents and gifts which thus far have been hidden from us.

14.   In the secular world, where care has been taken to ensure a healthy procedure, these things would be achieved by wide and effective advertising, by carefully monitored shortlisting procedures, by vigorous interviewing checked against reference, by medical and personality checks and by the ability to remove people whenever poor appointments are made. If the Church cannot have all of this, it has a special responsibility to consider how it intends to ensure the same outcome within its own system.

15.   There is an important presupposition here which holds that individuals can only make decisions about the future direction of their ministry if the corporate body of the Church is prepared to take the initiative. The Church calls. Individuals recognise the call and respond. Discerning the purpose of God is something worked out between the Church's sense of vocation and the individual so called. We cannot expect individuals to make up for any lack of vocational initiative and direction by the Church. That requires the Church to be clear what it is calling people to and why. It places a responsibility on the Church to ensure that the necessary support is given to ministries it calls into being. It would be no bad thing for the Church to have set out a clear agreed job description for all its senior posts. If this is to tune in with the sense of Christian vocation of those called, these statements of ministerial purpose need to be manifestly directed to the mission of the Gospel and the work of the Kingdom of God. This is where the common insights afforded to us in God's creation meet up with and join hands with the specific vision offered to the world in Jesus Christ. The Church and its ministry become a sign-post to the ultimate vision of a creation transformed and transfigured in Jesus Christ.

Things like job descriptions and systems of appraisal are

thereby turned to the highest purposes of enabling the Church to conduct a more effective and credible mission.

16.   All of this goes against the idea that appointments are made in some haphazard and amateurish way as the only way to leave the door open to the operation of the Holy Spirit. The serious business of seeking to understand the work of the Spirit requires the very best we can offer. It requires a Church which has a clear sense of the calling and responsibilities of its leaders, a recognition of the need for the highest known professionalism in seeking people to carry out these ministries and a resolute commitment to support and sustain both the institutions of ministry and the people called to fill them at any one time.

The Motion carried by the General Synod in July 1974 and the Prime Minister's Statement to the House of Commons in June 1976

1. The General Synod, in July 1974, carried a Motion in the following terms:

That the General Synod

i. affirms the principle that the decisive voice in the appointment of diocesan bishops should be that of the Church:

ii. believes that, in arrangements to give effect to this, it would be desirable that a small body, representative of the vacant diocese and of the wider Church, should choose a suitable person for appointment to that diocese and for the name to be submitted to the Sovereign, and

iii. instructs the Standing Committee to arrange for further consideration of these matters, including the administrative, legal and constitutional implications, and to report the results to the Synod at an early date.'

2. On Tuesday 8 June 1976 in a written Parliamentary Answer, the Prime Minister, Mr James Callaghan, made a statement in the following terms:

The Sovereign, who is herself the Supreme Governor of the established Church, appoints Archbishops and Diocesan Bishops on the advice of the Prime Minister of the day.

The House will know that there is some disquiet in the Church about the present system and that in 1974 the Church's General Synod passed a Motion affirming the principle that the decisive voice in the appointment of diocesan bishops should be that of the Church. As my predecessor informed the House on 24 February he held a number of talks, since that General Synod vote, with the Archbishop of Canterbury and Sir Norman Anderson, Chairman of the Synod's House of Laity. More recently I have discussed the matter with the

Archbishop of Canterbury and also with the leaders of the main Opposition parties, who have themselves had talks with the Archbishop and Sir Norman.

There are, in my view, cogent reasons why the State cannot divest itself from a concern with these appointments of the established Church. The Sovereign must be able to look for advice on a matter of this kind and that must mean, for a constitutional Sovereign, advice from Ministers. The archbishops and some of the bishops sit by right in the House of Lords, and their nomination must therefore remain a matter for the Prime Minister's concern. But I believe that there is a case for making some changes in the present arrangements so that the Church should have, and be seen to have, a greater say in the process of choosing its leaders.

As I see it, the main points of a new procedure might be as follows:-

Bishops and archbishops would continue to be appointed by the Queen. The Queen would continue to receive, as now, final advice from the Prime Minister on these appointments. In giving that final advice, the Prime Minister would retain a real element of choice.

To assess a vacancy and possible candidates for it, a small standing committee should be set up by the Church. The exact composition of such a committee remains to be settled, but it is envisaged that both the Prime Minister's secretary for appointments and the archbishops' appointments secretary, who will work in the fullest co-operation throughout, would be members of it.

The committee would draw up a short list of two names, which might be given in an order of preference. The Prime Minister would retain the right to recommend the second name, or to ask the committee for a further name or names.

A special procedure would be needed for the appointment of an Archbishop of Canterbury. The committee might then be chaired by a layman chosen by the Prime Minister.

Arrangements on these lines, which would not in themselves involve legislation, would give the Church a greater say in the choice of its leaders and at the same time would preserve the constitutional essentials of an established Church.

I hope therefore that these proposals, worked out after the consultations which I have mentioned and which are also supported by the leaders of the main Opposition parties, may commend themselves as settling this issue in a satisfactory way for the foreseeable future. The General Synod is due to discuss them next month, and that discussion will reflect what the mind of the Church on them may be.

APPENDIX VI

Guidelines for Appointing Groups

1. In Chapter 6 we propose processes for filling the various kind of posts in our remit. In the case of vacancies for suffragan bishops, deans and provosts we recommend that bishops making these appointments should be assisted by advice and recommendations from Appointing Groups. We say something about the make up of the Appointing Groups and their tasks and we touch on, *inter alia*, the issues of publicising vacancies, meeting the candidates and the prior consultations that will assist the Groups in their work. Issues of confidentiality are inherent in the process and need to be borne in mind. Some guidelines about all of these elements may be useful.

The Consultations

2. It is important to emphasise that each Group will decide what is the best method of consultation in its own circumstances on each occasion a vacancy arises. But there are some common elements. The Appointing Group will need to be well briefed at the outset about the context in which the post is being filled, and especially the members of the Group from outside the diocese. It will be useful at any early stage to identify for its secretary those issues relating to the job description about which he or she might make particular enquiries during the consultation. The secretary must be receptive to unexpected ideas coming forward. It will also be desirable at an early point to determine the form of the consultation: should some be in writing or all by interview? If by interview, should some people be seen one to one, or all in groups, and how much time should be allowed? - and so on.

3. For a suffragan bishopric the context might include matters that have been constant, irrespective of the particular incumbent, such as chairmanship of particular committees, oversight of particular subjects, care for specific groups of ministers, or kinds of ministry, or geographical areas or deaneries: what is the

'givenness' in the situation? For a dean or provost there may be responsibilities for exercising patronage, for serving on public bodies, and there may be limitations or opportunities determined by the statutes of the relevant cathedral: again it is what is constant whoever is the dean or provost of the day. Generally this material will be factual data rather than commentary or opinion.

4. As for the consultation, the aim is to gather advice from informed people, clergy and lay, the church and community, about their expectations of the office holder and the kind of person they hope to see appointed. In the case of a suffragan, his immediate colleagues are obviously to be consulted; and so, no doubt, are the Chairmen of the Houses of Clergy and Laity and members of the Bishop's Council; but depending on the actual post, chairmen of diocesan boards, sector ministers, other diocesan officials, rural deans and representatives of other ministers the bishop will be serving may all be appropriate. The choice of those to be consulted should reflect the links that the present or future suffragan has or will have, either in his own right or directly on behalf of the diocesan: they might include, for example, leading figures in other denominations, of other faiths, of major educational institutions or of industry or commerce or farming or tourism as appropriate. Relevance to the office holder's ministry will be the key test.

5. It will often be easier to identify the relevant people when a deanery or provostship is vacant because the majority of them will be the major figures in the civic life and community of the city in which the cathedral is set. But it could also be important to contact, for example, some of the leaders of organisations in the city and county that use the cathedral for major events and also those who play a considerable part supporting it.

6. The important point is to be seen to invite people's views: not all of them will respond, but better to throw the net widely at the risk of receiving too much advice than to risk attracting criticism by too limited an enquiry.

7. The aim of the consultation process is to enable the Appointing Group to feel confident that it can make recommen-

dations to the bishop that are well grounded in fact and well supported by real understanding of what people are seeking from the next ministry. Those who take part in this consultation will need to feel that their views are heard and respected. Inevitably advice will be received that cannot be adopted, and perhaps strong recommendations too, but whether they come from individuals or from groups, those offering them must feel that they have been properly considered.

8.   It may be the case that a member of the Appointing Group will be identified as one of the potential candidates to be considered for the appointment. When that occurs the member concerned should stand down as a member of the Appointing Group at the point that it becomes clear that his name is to be considered.

Publicising Vacancies

9.   Each Appointing Group will have to decide how to publicise the vacancy with which it is concerned. Very often it will be necessary to weigh up the advantages or disadvantages of full-blown advertising on the one part (notices in the Church press, and perhaps the national press, for example) and, on the other, more informal ways of seeking candidates. Public advertising has much to commend it in terms of fairness and openness but we are mindful, too, that in some traditions of the Church it has been and continues to be felt that putting one's name forward in response to an advertisement runs counter to the concept of being called to new work. Some of us regard it as a matter of principle that advertising should be used on every occasion in the light of the particular circumstances. Whatever the choice, it is important that it should be clear and highly desirable that it is well supported.

Meeting the Candidate

10.   We have also indicated that we recognise there are arguments for and against Appointing Groups, first, meeting candidates; second, formally interviewing them; and, third,

arranging for them to meet those with whom they would be working were they to be appointed. Most of us feel that there should on each occasion be some means by which the Appointing Group can meet the shortlisted candidates at least but we all recognise that a decision will be needed on each occasion whether to interview formally or not. Whichever approach is adopted, we believe it should be applied consistently to all candidates.

Confidentiality

11.   We consider that members of Appointing Groups must take the issue of confidentiality seriously. They may find, as members of the Crown Appointments Commission have done, that to give a public undertaking to one another in the meeting that they will not disclose what is said about candidates and by whom is a helpful means of guarding against loose talk. We have argued in all our proposals for greater openness in the application of the procedures and we hold to that. If the selection process chosen is a relatively open and competitive one, and especially if it follows public advertising, it may be thought that confidentiality is not an issue. In our view whatever the process, and however open it is, the content of the discussions about the candidates should not be discussed outside the meetings. When rumours fly, they can be very harmful and hurtful for the individual and those close to him or her. They can be harmful to the job the person currently occupies and even to that to which they might be going.

12.   Finally, as we have said earlier in this Report, it is axiomatic that the work of an Appointing Group is rooted in prayer. Even if the preferred appointing process mirrors secular practice in virtually every respect , it needs to be distinguished by continual recollection of the holy purpose that is being undertaken in this work.

APPENDIX VII

Memorandum of Dissent by Frank Field, MP

1. There is no dispute between members of the Working Party about the need to change the way the Crown makes appointments to senior positions in the Church. The present system – operating as it does in secret, dependent upon the old boy network, with candidates unaware even that they are being considered and the views of the interested parties channelled through a single person to the Prime Minister – may have been acceptable in Trollope's time. Today, however, it runs contrary to the commonly held view that appointments should be made in the open, that posts should be advertised, and that the very best use should be made of what talents are available. In all these respects the Church is at one with secular society.

2. All members of the Working Party also accept that the Established nature of the Church of England is one which has evolved, and continues to evolve. A key aspect of this Establishment status of the Church is the role the Crown enjoys in appointing to some senior Church positions. As the main report recalls, the role of the Crown in appointing diocesan bishops was radically changed in 1976. Where the Working Party and I part company is with regard to how the remaining system of Crown patronage should be changed. The Working Party argues, in effect, for its abolition, retaining the Monarch as a facade for the extent of the shift in power which it is actually proposing. While I argue for a radical reform of the present system I propose one which keeps the Crown's influence intact.

3. I believe the proposals made by the majority of the Working Party must necessarily raise the question of the Established position of the Church of England. For what would be left of the Crown's influence if the Government were to accede to the reforms in this report? And if the Crown were to lose its remaining influence in appointments how could the privileges of

the Church, particularly its endowments, remain intact? If the nation is to go down the road to disestablishment I believe we should do so only after a full and open debate and not as a consequence of other reforms. I leave for others to judge whether the Government believes that now is a necessary or appropriate time to change the position of the Monarch in respect to the Church of England or embark on a programme of disendowment.

4. In essence the differences within the Working Party are ecclesiological. The Working Party has a view of the Church of England as a sect. The key recommendation in the report is that a majority of places on any new advisory or appointments committee should go to those active in the Church. This approach ignores what the Church of England has meant to the English nation, and the response of ordinary citizens over the centuries. On the basis of attendance we have rarely been a church-going nation. Despite the penalties, large numbers refused to attend church even in medieval times. Failure to accept a set liturgical diet cannot be equated with disbelief. And yet this is precisely what is happening, and is best illustrated by the restriction a growing number of clergy now places on infant baptism. Moreover these restrictions, or signs of growing sectarianism, do not merely erect barriers between the Church and the nation, but ensure that fewer and fewer people understand what the Christian message is about. Unless the Church radically changes its approach we may now be living with the last generation which understands anything about the Christian message. Christian language is fast becoming a barrier to, rather than a conveyor of, meaning. While I do not for a single moment question the integrity of the members of the Working Party I believe their proposals will exacerbate this trend.

5. In practically all incidences the report only makes sense when referring to the Church if this concept is taken to mean the activists, and it is from this vision that, perhaps without realising it, the members are committed to a furtherance of sectarianism. All the arguments for change come from what I call the forces of Synod. Important as Synod is, it is not the Church of England. Rather it is an honest and human attempt to build a representative body of clergy and of those laity who are active in parish life.

6.   Yet even amongst active churchgoers most of the laity do not relate to Synod in any serious way, nor do they hold that body in the same high esteem as Synod members appear to do. Everything about the Church of England teaches that it is not owned by these activists. Throughout its history it has had a duty to the entire people of England, believers and non-believers, practising Anglicans and non-practising Anglicans alike. For most of the centuries since Christianity was established in this country the Crown has been the instrument through which the voice of the laity has been independent of the ecclesiastical establishment. In attempting to exclude or abolish Crown influence in senior appointments, the report, if accepted, will break that essential historic link between the Church and people which has been the dominant characteristic since the beginning of Christianity in this country one thousand seven hundred years ago.

7.   Although I believe it vital that the Crown link is maintained, the means by which the Crown exercises its influence calls out for reform. I believe the Crown's power should be exercised in public. I therefore endorse the appointments committee approach for senior positions. I do, however, believe that the majority of places on any such committee should go to Crown nominees. For this to be effective the Crown would need to appoint a group of people who would take the view of the wider Church which has been one of the aspects of the Crown's historic role in ecclesiastical appointments in this country. All these nominees need not be practising Anglicans. Under present arrangements, for example, for the appointment of a dean, the Patronage Secretary may consult the local leaders of other Christian denominations. Appointments to the new body of committed Christians from other denominations would also itself be a useful development in what we mean by Establishment in this country.

8.   One of the crucial defects of the Crown Appointments Commission which appoints diocesan bishops is its inability to make long-term plans for the career of senior clergy. With each diocesan appointment the Crown Appointments Commission changes; representatives of the local diocese come on to the Commission. While it is important that such representatives have

a say, their place on the Crown Appointments Commission makes it difficult, if not impossible, for the Commission to make a judgement about which people may be suitable for appointments which may occur over the next few years. The Commission is only able to consider a single appointment at any one time, and then its membership changes.

9.   The inherent weakness of being unable to make long-term plans in respect of senior appointments is unwittingly transferred by the new arrangements which the majority of the Working Party members propose; the membership of the appointment committee will totally change with each vacancy. Nor will the new system have available to it the same national view of the talent available as is currently, although imperfectly, realised through the Crown's Patronage Secretary. The only national view of candidates available, unless all posts are advertised, will come from the Archbishops' Appointments Secretary. The Working Party was reminded from evidence submitted to it of the shortcomings of relying on this single approach.

10.   It is important that this fundamental weakness of the Crown Appointments Commission is not reproduced in any new system. I propose a static group of Crown nominees who would automatically be members of any appointment committee for senior posts. The members from the local diocese should constitute less than a third of the membership so that the Crown nominees will be in a position to undertake long-term career planning in this area of Church appointments. The crucial difference with the present system, however, would be that the Crown would be exercising its influence in public, that the influence of the Patronage Secretary would be very much reduced, and that the decision of the appointing committee would be one which the Prime Minister automatically sends to the Monarch for approval.

11.   The report proposes that the Crown should lose its influence in the area of senior church appointments considered by the Working Party, while the reforms proposed here for the appointment of suffragan bishops would allow the Crown no place whatsoever. This is an unacceptable example of a

curtailment of pluralism in this country. And the reform is proposed despite the fact that the Working Party was presented with evidence to show that suffragan bishops were now the most important pool from which diocesan bishops are drawn. The Crown's presence on the appointing panel for a suffragan bishop should be a *quid pro quo* for opening up the Crown Appointments procedure along the lines I have suggested. Such a move would ensure that the wider Church's views were represented and that candidates not favoured by the hierarchy in Synod would be considered.

12.   It is because of the incomplete nature of any official list of what talent exists in the Church that I believe the report ought to advocate the general principle of advertising all senior posts unless a case can be made for employing some other approach. As this report stands the reverse applies; a case has to be made out for the post to be advertised. While any one approach by itself is inadequate, the invitation to apply, or the support of candidates by colleagues or by local congregations, is one way of ensuring that the Church's major resource, i.e. the men and women who serve it, is more adequately capitalised.

13.   While this issue of advertising is important it would not by itself warrant this dissenting note. The crucial issue in the fast-changing circumstances of today's world is the advantages which the current Establishment link offers the Church. It provides a national platform and a reminder of the Anglican Church's historic mission and responsibility to the entire nation. I believe that mission would be placed in further jeopardy if the recommendations of this report were to be enacted.

28 July 1992   Frank Field, MP